AFLOAT IN EUROPE

by the same author
Mariner in the Mediterranean

Afloat in Europe

BY JOHN MARRINER

ADLARD COLES LIMITED

First published in book form in 1967 by
Adlard Coles Ltd, 1–3 Upper James
Street, London W1, and printed in Great
Britain by W. & J. Mackay & Co Ltd,
Chatham, Kent © John Marriner 1967.

to my crews

without whom these wanderings could never have happened

Acknowledgements

I would like to acknowledge the kindness of the Editors of *The Yachting World*, *Yachting Monthly*, and *The Yachtsman* for allowing me to make use of material that has already appeared in their magazines.

But quite especially I offer my grateful thanks to Frank Snoxell, at that time in the editorial chair of *The Motor Boat and Yachting*, and who first had the courage to put my yachting tales into print, and to Erroll Bruce, his successor in that chair, for his help and encouragement to go ahead with this book.

Contents

List of Illustrations

List of Maps

Foreword

I have been meaning to write this book for years. I bought my first motor yacht in 1952: she was fairly awful, a converted Admiralty harbour launch of 36 feet in length and with a petrol motor that finally blew up and landed me with a constructive total loss right in the middle of my home port of St Helier, in Jersey. She was called *Barracuda* and her mangled hull still rots here on my doorstep.

With the money from Lloyd's, I bought a steel boat built in the Netherlands, which I called *Dame des Iles*, after a large craft that some friends and I used to drive around the Channel Islands for filthy lucre. Incidentally, in medieval times, this was a sinecure job connected with the islands. I loved the old *Dame* dearly, swearing that I would never buy another boat until I was offered too tempting a price to refuse.

So along came *September Tide*. I called her this because of the play, because I was getting to that time in my own yachting life. The tides are highest that month.

My boat has taken me almost everywhere I want to go in a motor yacht, though there are still just one or two places to explore before we lay up.

We have made lots of friends on passage; and they often ask what it was like in the places we have been to—so this is really just me telling them.

Jersey 1966

1
Grand Tour through Europe

First-class Return through France, Switzerland,
Germany and the Netherlands

Many people of more vivid imagination than myself have written of the beauties and interest of the French inland waterways. I do not propose to do so: I want only to give some practical advice on getting from the English Channel to the Mediterranean, based on my own experiences in *Dame des Iles*, a 48 ft motor yacht with a beam of 11 ft, a 4 ft 6 in. draught and a steel hull.

The best months for navigating the French waterways are April, May and June. July and August should be avoided, as there are periods then when they clean out sections of each canal—called *chômages*—and these may seriously hold you up. September—unless it has rained a lot—may be a month of low water in the canals and rivers, which thus become difficult to navigate.

The official agencies issue instructions telling you what papers you need. We went to considerable trouble to do the right thing in advance. So far as we were concerned, it seemed a waste of time. All you needed was the usual Certificate of Registry, your passport and a *Certificat de Capacité*. Everything else you could obtain in Rouen, or at whatever other port you might enter the inland waterways. On arrival at this port of entry you were given a *laissez-passer* by the Customs, who also checked the stores in the usual way and stamped your passport.

At Le Havre, our own last port before going up the Seine to Rouen, we shipped a quantity of spirits, wines and tobacco at duty-free prices. The Customs men at Rouen were most helpful about all this. There was no attempt to seal us; we were merely told that, on arrival at Marseille, we would be required to show all that we had on board at Rouen, less a reasonable amount for consumption on passage. This was noted on our *laissez-passer* and that was all there was to it. In fact, no one at Marseille asked to see our stores.*

With fuel, the matter was rather more tricky. There are not many motor yachts which can guarantee to make the passage across France on the fuel in their tanks. Mindful of this, we asked the score in Le Havre, and the ship chandler—rather too good a salesman—sold us two large drums of Esso diesel fuel, which we stowed on the quarter-deck and lashed down. We did not look very nice with these aboard, but it had to be. They cost us the ordinary duty-free price, whereas the inland price which we would have had to pay if we had bought them when once technically 'inside' France would have been at least double. The ship chandler assured us that we would have no Customs worries on declaring them. At Rouen, however, we were asked some rather searching questions about the amount of fuel in these drums and what sort it was. The rule is that you can carry as much as you like in your tanks, but that everything stowed elsewhere must pay duty. It was only due to the good sense of the Customs men that we managed to get away with these drums and one must not bank on being able to do so again. Incidentally, we were told by our ship-chandler friend that one could get rid of the drums—against repayment of one's deposit— at any garage. Our own experience was that only Esso agents would accept Esso drums, only Shell agents Shell drums, and so on; and then only at towns of the size of Lyon or Marseille. Our drums stayed with us like old men of the sea, ugly and stubborn, till we got to Lyon.

One should stock up, before sailing, with as many canned goods as possible, as these are absurdly expensive in France; that goes for soap and Nescafé, too. But, at least in the central areas, bread, milk, eggs, vegetables and even cream were surprisingly cheap and could be bought from every

* I am sorry to say that, since 1955, things have tightened up quite a lot. One is no longer allowed to take one's stores with one as in the good old days: only sufficient for the journey is left aboard, the remainder having to be shipped by a transit agent to Marseille, where it has to be cleared aboard again. These changes have been brought about by a number of yachts 'cheating' and financing their trip by selling their duty-free things *en route* at local prices. So the innocent must suffer with the guilty—one can have little sympathy with the naughty boys.

lock-keeper. If you are a drinker of things like tonic-water, ginger-ale or Coca-Cola, you should also buy these before you start, to avoid ruin *en route*.

Always assuming that you go first to Paris—much the most practical way of doing things—there are subsequently several routes which a yacht can successfully take. The most important three are:

(*a*) Up the Seine past Melun as far as St Mammès, where you enter the Canal du Loing. Thence by several intercommunicating canals as far as Chalon-sur-Saône, where you enter the River Saône, which in turn joins the River Rhône at Lyon, thence to the sea. This is known as the Bourbonnais route and is recommended by the Touring Club de France. It is probably the longest of the three, but has the least locks, though some are pretty ancient. It is the route we took in 1955.

(*b*) Up the Seine to a point just above St Mammès, thence into the long Canal de Bourgogne, through Dijon and into the River Saône at St Jean de Losne. Thence as in (*a*) above. This is known as the Burgundy route. It looks a bit shorter than (*a*) on the map, but has the most locks.

(*c*) From Paris take the Marne and the Canal Latéral à la Marne and then the Canal de la Marne à la Saône, which ultimately joins the River Saône at Heuilley. This is probably the easiest of the routes from a locking point of view, but it is more industrialized and the French clubs try to persuade you not to use it.

The following limitations as to a yacht's measurements apply to all of the Seine routes through France:

Length	126 ft $3\frac{3}{4}$ in. (38.5 m.)
Draught	5 ft $10\frac{7}{8}$ in. (1.8 m.)
Beam	16 ft $4\frac{7}{8}$ in. (5 m.)
Height above waterline	11 ft 6 in. (3.5 m.)

My own experience is that a maximum draught of 5 ft 10 in. or so is a bit generous. We only drew about 4 ft 6 in. and at some points in the canals we found ourselves touching the mud. This may, however, have been due to the wake of the vessel drawing down her stern in the shallow water.

How can our experiences most help others? Maybe the best way to do this is simply to recount the log in an abbreviated form:

At 1200 on April 16, 1955, we sailed from Jersey and made Cherbourg

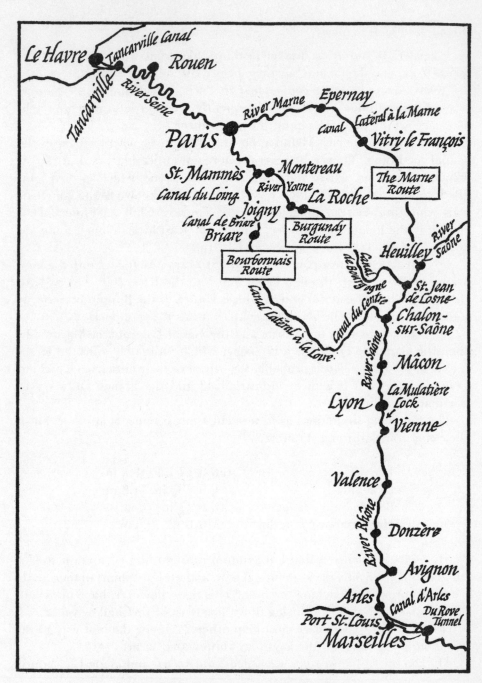

1. The three main routes south through France

about 1900. On April 20, after something of a buffeting in the Baie de la Seine, we made Le Havre and embarked stores and fuel.

Scorning the Tancarville Canal, we took the evening tide up the estuary past Honfleur, soon after which we caught the flood tide up to Caudebec, which we reached in the dark. As we were going alongside for the night, we were caught by the bore (*le mascaret*) and sustained damage aft. One has to pay for one's inexperience. The damage was put right next day at Rouen, where Customs were cleared and we officially entered the French inland waterways. A further three days of fairly hard steaming—with eight locks to pass, but all easy ones—saw us made fast at the hospitable Paris Yacht Harbour. For those who do not already know, it is situated close to the Pont Alexandre III and is officially known as Touring Club de France, Port de Plaisance de Paris, Quai de la Conférence, Paris 8. The telephone number is Anjou 2880—you may have your own telephone extension installed aboard—and the people there look after yachts extremely well. There were no more formalities to complete if you had already gone through the drill at Rouen and obtained your *laissez-passer*.

We took the Bourbonnais route, as recommended to us by the Touring Club de France. Before dealing with the actual journey through the inland waterways, there are a few points that may be mentioned regarding crew, manners and regulations.

I have heard of a friend of mine who took his auxiliary sailing ketch south through the canals with only himself and a hand aboard, but they regretted their foolhardiness later on and got little pleasure from it. In the average cruiser, a crew of four is desirable: one at the wheel, one forward and one aft at each lock, and one to cook and maybe give a hand generally. For one has to keep going pretty well all the time, so as not to lose one's place in the stream of traffic. This may be a psychological weakness in human character—one could, of course, stop and take the whole thing more easily—but one somehow doesn't stop and hates to think of losing one's place in the line.

Generally speaking, a vessel must keep to the right in the canals, but there are a few occasions when this rule must be broken. If, for instance, the towpath is only on one side of the canal and this causes a vessel under tow to be on the wrong side, a powered vessel must allow a barge under tow to proceed, taking action to avoid interference with the towing mechanism, be it motor or mule. On the whole, the barge skippers are extremely polite and helpful. Even important diesel-driven barges will stop and allow themselves to be overtaken if you give a sound signal. Sometimes a skipper does not like to be overhauled if he is approaching a lock, but the strict rule is that you may overtake until a sign appears on your starboard hand indicating that the overtaking limits (*Limites de Trématage*) have been reached. This is usually about 50 yards before a lock gate.

Hours of navigation in summer are from about 0630 until 1930. If you want to pass a lock after navigation has ceased—provided it is not altogether too late and the lock family is already at its evening meal—you can usually get away with it by tipping the lock-keeper.

What follows will give you a good idea of what happened in 1955 on our trip down the rivers and canals.

April 30. We slipped from Paris Yacht Harbour at 0940 and went up the Seine for a distance of some 35 sea-miles to Melun, where we made fast at the Rowing Club for two nights. The scenery was perfectly lovely all the way and the locks fully manned, so that we had nothing to do ourselves. The waits at the locks were rather long, as the keepers often had to wait for traffic that had been signalled to them in advance. Much of the trip was made in company with the small British motor yacht *Anamac*, belonging to the Macmillan brothers. During this day we passed seven locks. At Melun we were compelled to spend the whole of May 1, Labour Day, as this is a public holiday in France and the locks are not manned.

May 2. We slipped early—at 0635—and continued until 1855. We had previously decided to have a system of a 'hard' day with early rising, no stops for meals and pressing on until last light, followed by an 'easy' day, getting up late, often stopping for meals and finishing when we felt like it. A little before midday we left the River Seine and entered the Canal du Loing at St Mammès, where we decided not to buy the long poles (price Frs 1,000 each) which were on sale for fending us off the canal sides at night. With our small draught of 4 ft 6 in. we could lie close enough alongside—there being no movement—for it not to matter. If necessary, we could use a couple of boathooks to keep us off. Our first day in the canals went a lot better than we had hoped, although the strong wind was a bit tiresome at some of the locks. We decided, for the sake of exercise more than anything else, to start a drill at locks. I remained at the wheel, Ted jumped ashore to help the lock staff make fast, George and Peg took warps at each end and made fast inboard. When we were fast, I often went ashore and gave a hand with the shutting and opening of the gates, leaping back aboard when the moment came to push off. This drill, with modifications, we operated all the way through the canals, and I think it worked in very well with the lock staffs, who were duly grateful. Of course, the locks at present and—with few exceptions—until we reached Le Creusot in the Canal du Centre, were ascending. This day we did 38 sea-miles and passed sixteen locks.

May 3. An 'easy' day. We covered 20 sea-miles and seventeen locks. At lunch-time, we passed through Buges Junction locks and out of the Canal du Loing—so called from the River Loing that feeds it—into the Canal de Briare. Not very much traffic was encountered, and it was mostly horse and mule drawn. We spent the night at Montbouy, having lunched well at Montargis.

May 4. A 'hard' day from 0717 to 1955. In the forenoon we passed Rogny, with its disused but famous series of Seven Locks (Les Sept Ecluses) leading one into the other with a total rise of 35 metres. Built by Sully in 1605, they were in use until 1887. It made us think. Soon afterwards, at La Javacière, we stopped ascending locks from the Seine level and started descending locks towards the Loire level. At 1600 we passed over the famous canal bridge, which carries the canal over the River Loire, a unique experience. Starting at 0500, the bridge is opened to southbound traffic only for $2\frac{1}{2}$ hours, then for $2\frac{1}{2}$ hours to northbound, and so on through the day until 2000. Fortunately, we arrived during a southbound period and passed unhindered. At this point, the Canal de Briare joins the long and relatively lock-free Canal Latéral à la Loire. During the afternoon we passed the British motor yacht *Forge*, belonging to Miss Dorrien-Smith and Mrs Williams and were delighted to exchange greetings. They were on their way south to look at the flamingos in the Camargue. This day we passed through twenty-six locks and covered 39 sea-miles, stopping the night at Les Fouchards, near Cosne.

May 5. An 'easy' day, with a pleasant stop for lunch. We nevertheless covered 28 sea-miles and passed eleven locks, making fast for the night close to the double locks and canal bridge at Le Guétin. The canal became more industrialized.

May 6. After some argument with the lock-keepers due to a misunderstanding over permissible times of passage, we were locked into the Le Guétin double locks and crossed the Canal Bridge over the River Allier with *Forge*. After a 'hard' day ending at 1915, we made fast for the night at Garnat, having done 36 sea-miles and passed thirteen locks. *Forge* had left the main canal, taking the turning up to Nevers.

May 7. As it was Saturday and we wanted to shop in Digoin, we started early—at 0705—and had arrived at Digoin by soon after lunch, having done 22 sea-miles and passed nine locks. At Digoin, where we left the Canal Latéral à la Loire to join the Canal du Centre, we watered and transferred fuel oil from our deck containers to tanks. From Digoin onwards, the locks on the Canal du Centre are numbered 28, 27, etc., Ocean, indicating a fall of water towards the Atlantic, and farther on, from Le Creusot, 1, 2, 3, etc., Mediterranean, indicating a flow towards the Mediterranean. We tried to get rid of our two Esso containers, but the fuel station here refused to take them.

May 8. This day being a Sunday, the Canal du Centre was full of barge traffic. As there is no stevedoring on Sundays, the skippers like to get under way and not waste time. This canal is relatively narrow, turns are frequent and industry is the keynote, though there are also patches of lovely country. We covered 26 miles and seventeen locks before the swing bridge at Montceau-les-Mines barred our way and we spent the night in fully industrial surroundings among cheerful mining folk. Montceau is an important barge port, accommodating as many as fifty-five barges in its basins.

May 9. A 'hard' day and a memorable one. Casting off at 0650, by 1100 we were at Le Creusot, the stretch of canal between Lock No. 1 Ocean and Lock No. 1 Mediterranean and the highest point reached (301.08 metres above sea-level). Here are the twin lakes of La Muette and Montchanin, whose spring-fed waters aliment the Canal du Centre as it flows downhill towards Atlantic and Mediterranean. So it is not an unimportant place. From then onwards all the locks we passed were descending, a matter for rejoicing. At 1910 we made fast for the night at St Léger after a gruelling day of twenty-six locks, covering only 15 sea-miles. At Long Pendu—soon after Le Creusot—there had been no fewer than eight locks, one after the other, all in a series downhill. We renewed our Calor gas cylinder.

May 10. This was an 'easy' day and one that saw the last of the canals of France on this trip. Casting off at 0940 and stopping for lunch, we arrived in the River Saône at Chalon-sur-Saône at 1820 and moored gratefully alongside the Quai Gambetta. Today we had covered 17 sea-miles and passed through eighteen locks. The canal was full of curves, but seemed to have more water in it than on the previous two days.

May 11. In Chalon we again tried without success to get a refund on our two empty fuel drums. Observing how slow was the Saône current, we refused the services of the pilots (thus saving some Frs 8,000) and set off after lunch with the aid of our river plan which we had bought in Paris. Navigation was easy, the main, but easily avoided, danger being the dykes containing the principal channel of the river. We spent the night at Macon, some 31 sea-miles below Chalon, there having been only one lock to negotiate. It had rained all day.

May 12. A delightful sunny morning. We started off at 0935, lunched alongside at Trévoux and were joined in the Bernalin locks by the Norwegian motor yacht *Navajo V*, which had come from Oslo, via the Rhine and the Rhine-Rhône Canal. We had grounded just before this lock—only gently—on some mud, due to a slight inaccuracy in the river plan, which indicates that you should hold to the middle channel, whereas the true channel is on the left going downstream. As *Navajo* had a pilot aboard, we let her go ahead after the next lock and, passing through some very lovely river scenery, arrived at Lyon (Pont Tilsitt) at 1720, having covered 40 sea-miles from Mâcon and passed through four locks. It had been a really pleasant day. In Lyon, where we spent two nights, we at last got our money back from Esso on the two empty drums, had some laundry done rather expensively and went to have a look at our next enemy, the Rhône. I telephoned the author of the excellent Rhône plan and asked him his advice about taking a pilot. He replied that the plan was dead accurate, but asked me whether I thought we would really have the time, in this fast-flowing river, to make out the leading marks. I had to admit that this seemed very doubtful, and thankfully we engaged Joseph Pariset, a pilot who had presented himself aboard meanwhile.

May 14. The pilot boarded us soon after 0530 and, after an irritating wait at the great locks of La Mulatière, we eventually found ourselves in the Rhône at 0735. It was at once obvious that we had done right to take a pilot. We were surrounded by swirling whirlpools and rapids. If we had

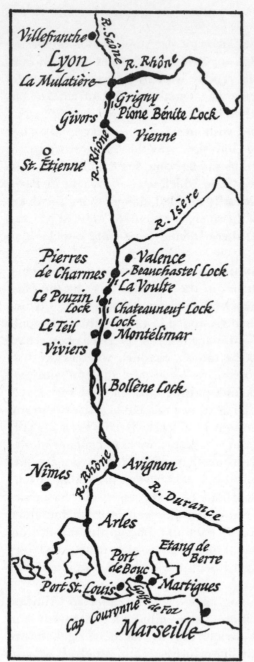

not had Pariset with us, I would immediately have gone alongside the nearest quay and telephoned for help. When we made this trip in 1955, 1957, and again in 1960, it was still optional whether one took a pilot on the Rhône or not. I have heard that since then it has been made compulsory, in view of the number of accidents that used to happen. The pilotage fee from Lyon to Arles used to be in the neighbourhood of NF. 120, but I hear that, like most things, this has also risen slightly. Whatever it is, it is well worth paying.

At times the river ran with a speed of about 6–7 knots, though there were many stretches where it was not more than 2–3 knots. Ascending barges must be passed on the side on which they expose a dark blue flag. Descending traffic has priority and it is the duty of a descending vessel to sound her siren as she passes certain places where a look-out is stationed. This look-out telephones to the next narrows downstream, warning the look-out there to detain all upstream traffic until the vessel in question has passed down. At 1550 we entered the fine broad new canal

2. *The Rhône*

which leads from Donzère to Mondragon, lower down the river, and half an hour later were in the amazing new Bollène Locks, the deepest in Europe at 26 metres (over 85 ft). A giant hydro-electric station lies next to them.

This is the first of some fourteen projects which are destined to canalize much of the Rhône in years to come and which will perhaps restore to the river much of its lost maritime trade. The primary object of the scheme is, however, to provide power stations from which a great volume of France's electricity will derive. Pariset, exhausted, slept while we were in the canal, and I took over until we rejoined the river. At 1935 we were fast at the lovely town of Avignon, with the Rhône racing by at some 5–6 knots.

Pariset told us that our craft, whose maximum effective speed was 9 knots, would be able to ascend the Rhône from Arles to Lyon in a matter of about five days. Pilotage would be Frs 7,000 a day and we would have to reckon on fuel consumption at top speed for some 12 hours a day. It seemed to me it might be cheaper to cadge a tow at a figure of somewhere between Frs 70,000 and Frs 100,000 (a matter of three days) and have no fuel expenditure, and, what was more important, much less worry. Some friends of ours in their 10-knot H.D.M.L. conversion *Wendala* came back up the Rhône that autumn and had a most anxious time with their pilot, who almost had a nervous breakdown.

From Lyon to Avignon was 135 sea-miles.

May 16. After two nights in Avignon, we cast off the following day at 1433, with a pilot named Laurent aboard, who was deputizing for Pariset. This excellent man took us safely down to Arles, which we reached at 1630, after having done a lockless stretch of 22 sea-miles. The current, which had been decreasing throughout this passage, was almost negligible at Arles.

May 17. It had come on to blow from the southward and our berth was becoming uncomfortable. So at 1730 we sailed from Arles and fought our way down the broad river against the short steep seas. We had to reduce speed to avoid damage and did not make Port St Louis until 2015. We had been warned not to attempt any direct passage seaward through the estuary owing to the constantly shifting sandbanks and the shallow waters. Only local fishermen ever use the estuary. We again covered 22 sea-miles.

May 18. After a very early argument with an official who vainly tried to eject us from the lock where we were lying, we passed through it at 0715 and made fast for the forenoon in the town basin. Port St Louis is small and

very unattractive and we were glad to sail at 1235 and pass down the broad
and short Port St Louis canal to the Golfe de Fos, where we at last found
ourselves in the blue waters of the Mediterranean. As it was still blowing
strongly, we decided to abandon our project of making Marseille by passing outside Cap Couronne, and instead steered east across the Golfe de Fos
for Port de Bouc. By this route the distance from Port St Louis to Marseille
is 29 sea-miles. Here we entered a channel leading to Martigues, where
there was a swing bridge. On the other side we had the choice of entering
the great refinery-rimmed lake known as the Etang de Berre or branching
to starboard into the Canal du Rhône, which we did. An hour later and
the entrance to the great Tunnel du Rove was ahead of us. We switched on
our searchlight and started an hour's gloomy passage through this engineer-
ing marvel. There is one-way traffic, controlled at each end, and the tunnel,
which stretches for five miles, is dead straight, so that you can see the other
end throughout. It is unlighted. It took us an hour to pass through. At the
other end, we made fast and raised our mast, the first time since we left
Paris. After an unpleasant three-quarters of an hour crossing the Gulf of
Marseille, we at length made fast at 1910 in a howling *mistral* in the Vieux
Port of Marseille, dirty but proud. We were really in the Med.

Summary

Le Havre to Marseille	.. ..	21 sailing days
Distance covered	.. .. ..	769 sea-miles (1,425 kilometres)
Locks negotiated	.. .. ..	175
Fuel consumed	.. .. ..	300 gallons of diesel oil

Approximate cost (not counting drink or amusements ashore):   £   s.

	£	s.
Four persons fed for, say, 21 days at, say, 12s. 6d. each per diem	47	5
307 gallons of diesel fuel, i.e. 1,381½ litres at, say, Frs 20 per litre Frs 27,630	28	0
Tips to lock-keepers, etc., say	2	0
Charts, plans, etc., other than those borrowed or already aboard	2	0
Dues in Paris, say	1	0
Fresh water, say	2	0

	£	s.
Lubricating oil consumed, say	2	0
Rhône pilotage (with tip)	13	0
Laundry, say	10	0
Calor gas consumed, say	4	0
Cleaning materials, say	1	0
Total £112	112	5

NOTE: Running repairs, which in our unlucky case totalled some £30, are not included.

In October 1956 I decided it was time the *Dame des Iles* came home again.

When I first brought her down to the Mediterranean in 1955, I found things there less expensive than I had been led to believe and soon gained the impression that I was in a sort of yachtsman's financial paradise. It was a fool's paradise. By summer of my second season in the Mediterranean I realized that—to a Provençal at least—the possession of such a luxury as a yacht marks you down as easy prey. Prices, I finally decided, were at least double what they were at home and the people less scrupulous. The work, too, left much to be desired. There seemed, therefore, no good reason to winter down there when one could easily negotiate the European waterways homewards. So off we started.

Jersey, my home port, was our goal. Why go the usual canal routes? We had done these the year before. This time I was bent on a journey up the Rhône, across to Switzerland and down the Rhine.

The immediate problem was how to get up the Rhône as far as Lyon. My excellent Cannes agent, Monsieur Glémot, had been doing his best to find out for me, but with his characteristic honesty had advised me it might be better to go and find out for myself. France is in many respects a curiously decentralized country: Official information on which one can rely is very hard to come by and even commercial 'know-how' of the type we required is often unreliable and subject to frequent change at the whim of the man on the spot. It therefore seemed very wise to go to Marseille and find out for oneself.

Some friends of mine who had come up the Rhône under their own

power in their 10-knot motor yacht the year before had told me that they
seemed to have very little power in reserve. It had, they admitted, been
a nerve-racking experience and one they would not care to repeat—
even with the same competent pilot. My own yacht, with a dirty end-of-
season bottom, could not be relied on for more than 8½ knots at full revs,
and I had read in an English handbook that one needed at least 12 knots
under one's own power to make the ascent. Now that I know more about
it, I think that is an exaggeration: 10 knots should, I think, warrant the
attempt. But 8½ is, I think, dangerously little.

Marseille is not much of a port for a yacht. We were champing at the bit
to get away from the place. But first we had to find out something about
the way to Lyon.

My first act was to telephone my old friend Joseph Pariset, the Rhône
pilot who had brought us down from Lyon to the sea the year before. He
had tested our boat in the narrows at Avignon against the current and
remembered it. Pariset did his best to persuade me not to try for a tow, but
to take him on as pilot and go on under our own power. This, he explained,
was our cheapest way up the river, and his fee would not exceed Frs 35,000,
together, of course, with his keep. He estimated that we would be able to
get from Arles to Lyon in five or six days.

I was tempted by Pariset's offer. It would be nice to see him again and
this would certainly be a cheap enough way of travelling. But there was
the fuel to consider: I took out a pencil and a piece of paper. Say 3 gallons
of diesel oil for 10 hours a day for 6 days at Frs 20 per litre (or Frs 90 a
gallon). This would cost about Frs 16,000 and I would have a nearly empty
tank on arrival, instead of a full one. I had, moreover, been told that, once
in the internal waterway of France, we would have to pay the full inland
price for our fuel.

Reggie Paul and Jim Newnham, who were my long-suffering crew at the
time, decided it for me by saying that, as far as they were concerned, safety
must come first. And so it came about that, over a Pernod in the Vieux
Port, we sent Pariset a postcard regretting that we had not the power to
make use of his offer.

My Cannes agents had written some weeks before to one of the biggest
of the Rhône hauliers, the Citerna concern, asking for their rates to give me
a tow to Lyon. It was, however, in true local tradition that when I called

at their offices in Marseille, Citerna knew nothing about me. After some argument, however, they quoted me a rate of tow of Frs 80,000 if— and a big 'if' it seemed—they had a suitable vessel for the job. They did not seem at all keen, and rather than become importunate, I went along to the offices of the rival concern, the Compagnie Générale de Navigation Havre, Paris, Lyon, Marseille (known as the H.P.L.M.), and there found a much kinder reception. Monsieur Tardieu, the local director, was something of a sportsman who enjoyed helping little boats and I was not surprised when, next morning, a letter arrived from him saying that his company was prepared to tow me up the Rhône to Lyon from Arles, whither I should proceed forthwith.

It is only fair to mention, at this point, that we had already been in correspondence with an excellent man, Monsieur R. Olivier, the proprietor of a stout Rhône barge and resident in Lyon. He is always known as most helpful to yachts needing a tow and it was only the fact that his journeys up and down the Rhône did not entirely fit in with our own time-table that prevented us from accepting his kind offer. His fee was Frs 70,000 for the Arles-Lyon tow. And he is his own master, so that he does not suffer from the 'We will ask our Head Office at Lyon' complex that Citerna and H.P.L.M. have to suffer.

As soon as we received H.P.L.M.'s welcome offer, we rang them up to accept and slipped immediately. It was the afternoon of October 14, 1956. The sea was calm and we enjoyed a pleasant trip coastwise outside Cap Couronne into the Golfe de Fos and along the canal to Martigues. No sooner had we made fast than the usual official requests to berth elsewhere became apparent. Since we were at the same time enveloped in a thick cloud of mosquitoes, we turned tail and fled back along the canal to Port de Bouc, where we hoped to fuel for the last time at cheap rates next morning. The mosquitoes, we afterwards learned, breed in the Etang de Berre next to Martigues and become insupportable at sunset.

Port de Bouc is not exactly a jolly place. But we managed to fill our tanks with diesel oil at sea-going rates (Frs 17 a litre here) before sailing. We had to swear that we were putting to sea and not entering the inland waterways. Apparently, the passage across the Golfe de Fos counts as 'sea', and well it might have that morning, as it was extremely rough.

We made Port St Louis, where one officially enters the Rhône, at lunch-time, and I went ashore prepared for much argument. The local officials, however, were in light-hearted mood and there was no Customs examination of any kind. The Customs *laissez-passer*, valid for one month (price Frs 1,200), was made out immediately and I was told to get on with it. They are used to yachts here. I visited the harbour master to pay my respects and ask for a 'Permis de Circulation', but he was out of the official forms and suggested I ask on arrival at Arles. While we were chatting, the man who worked the lock into the river arrived and darkly hinted that, if I liked to pay an extra Frs 520, I could lock through at once.

The Rhône from Arles to Port St Louis runs slowly and the channel is wide. A vessel drawing up to 6 ft should be able to make it easily without a pilot in either direction by using common sense and keeping to the outer sweep of the curves. It is not a pretty stretch of river and there is not much traffic. We reached Arles about 1600 and made fast in pouring rain alongside a H.P.L.M. barge, fatuously hoping that this might be our companion upriver.

I went ashore at once and visited the offices—on the Trinquetaille side of the river—of Monsieur Paris, the local agent of H.P.L.M., all prepared to apologize for being late. I need not have bothered. Monsieur Paris was in no hurry. The barge designated to tow us up had just gone downstream to Port St Louis, where he was to load, and was not expected to leave Arles for a couple of days. At that very moment a fellow I knew from Cannes came into the office and proudly announced that the *Massilia*, the Citerna company's flagship, was towing him up to Arles the next morning.

Our next call had to be at the Office National de la Navigation (Director: M. J. Dayre), where we were kindly received by a patient '*fonctionnaire*', who gave us a mystic piece of paper—in lieu of our 'Permis de Circulation', which, he explained, we could pick up in Lyon. There was, for once, no attempt to extract money. Monsieur Paris had meanwhile given me his receipt for the Frs 70,000 which was his company's fee for the tow.

Two maddening days went by, after which M. Paris arranged for us to get our tow next morning from the large Rhône barge *C.N.R.3*, which was sailing for Lyon at 0600. C.N.R. stands for Compagnie Nationale du Rhône, a State company that exploits the river for the public benefit.

C.N.R.3 was under charter to its managers, the H.P.L.M. She was a shallow-draught barge with two sixteen-cylinder Baudouin diesels giving her over 1,000 h.p. and had a total length of about 150 ft, I should say.

Thick fog, the bugbear of the river people, delayed our sailing 4 hours until nearly 1000, when we at last slipped, made fast alongside *C.N.R.3*, a steel tow rope and one of our own warps forward and two warps aft. We left our gears in neutral, thinking to help, but the infuriating noise they made soon taught us to engage the forward gear.

The skipper of the *C.N.R.3* was a delightful fellow known to us simply as 'Monsieur'. He had a jolly wife on board, who insisted on doing ironing and washing for us, and a very noisy granddaughter. He had a crew of two men and a boy. No one seemed to have any special duties, but everything functioned smoothly and happily. Most evenings we had a get-together in the *C.N.R.3*'s most spacious living-quarters, where we were regaled with home-made Pernod made out of a packet (not always very nice). *C.N.R.3* usually had at least one large barge in tow and the crews used to join in the fun whenever 'Monsieur' invited them.

We were greatly struck the whole journey by the way the skipper took his responsibilities. It is a colossal strain to be at the wheel all day, without a break, in the conditions one finds on the river. The great wheel has to be attended to all the time; there is the additional worry of the steel towing hawser, which has to be extended or taken in as conditions demand, and all the while the river channel must be followed with absolute accuracy or the whole convoy might go aground. Many times I noted the sweat on 'Monsieur's' sun-tanned brow, as I watched in silent sympathy.

That same evening we made Avignon. 'Monsieur' had asked me to run my engines full ahead to take some of the load off him as we approached the famous bridge, where the current must have been running at about 6 knots, and I was glad to see our forward tow line slacken as the strain eased. Making fast was a miracle of 'river seamanship'. *C.N.R.3* just put her bow in and threw a line over a bollard and there we were for the night. I did not even have to let go, although I was inboard of her great bulk. Of course, she was at a considerable angle to the quay. There was a small American yacht alongside, on her way downstream.

There was a great family reunion at Avignon, where 'Madame's' family mostly lived. The Palais des Papes was lit up and the whole fairy-tale city was, as usual, alive with its unreal combination of past and present.

Fog again next morning, but we got away at 0800, slipped our barge at
a factory quay a few miles upriver (another miracle of navigation) and
there followed a few anxious miles. *C.N.R.3*'s crew all went forward with
poles, sounding the depth, sometimes for half an hour at a time. There is
quite a language of signs between the forecastle and the bridge to show how
much water there is. Depths are expressed in metres and centimetres: the
number of fingers held up first shows the metres, a sweep of the arm means
50 centimetres and the next lot of fingers more centimetres. If there is no
sweep of the arm, the next lot of fingers simply shows the centimetres. I
have seen the Austrian and Hungarian bargees do just the same thing on
the Danube.

That afternoon about half past four we arrived at the Bollène locks, the
largest in Europe. There were some adjustments going on, so we were
asked if we minded waiting on the downstream side until the morning. As
we were in any case not going farther than Bollène that night, *C.N.R.3*'s
skipper, as commodore of our little convoy, agreed.

It was still dark next morning as we entered the lock. On the other side
we caught a glimpse of a brand-new German motor yacht, the *Kormoran*,
built for a Dr Projahn, of Düsseldorf. She was being piloted down the
Rhône by my old friend Pariset, with whom I had spent the previous
evening in the one pub that Bollène boasted. She was long and low and
painted black, evidently designed for cruising the waterways of Europe
with the least trouble.

At Viviers, about 3 hours upstream from the lock, we took another
Rhône barge, the petrol tanker *Forbin* and a dumb-barge in tow. The river-
men knew that the *Forbin* would not be able to get past the strong run of
current at Km. 150 (upriver from Le Teil) with her tow, so that our services
were enlisted to this effect. Indeed, when we reached this notorious kilometre sign (the whole Rhône is marked in kilometres from Lyon to Port
St Louis), although we were ourselves helping by running our motors full
ahead, our convoy of *C.N.R.3*, *Forbin*, the dumb-barge and ourselves made
good only one knot over the ground between Km. 150 and Km. 148, where
we again entered calmer water. The strength of the current here could be
accurately gauged at 8 knots.

There was a man standing on the bank at Le Pouzin (about Km. 136) with a signal asking us if we would care to relinquish our tow, but our commodore refused. He must have regretted his gesture, for soon afterwards he developed trouble with the injectors of his port motor and had to slip his tow. We made fast at La Voulte (Km. 127) at 1830.

The next day—our fourth under tow—was the hardest for our convoy. We had made an early start (at 0620) with both barges again in tow. Soon after 0700 I was asked to run my motors for half an hour and again at Km. 119—the celebrated Pierres de Charmes—we again started up at full revs. To my horror, I realized after half an hour's battling with the current, that we were making absolutely no headway. *C.N.R.3*'s skipper, his face very naturally running with sweat, asked me to stop my motors. He himself slackened speed and we started to drift slowly back with the current. After retreating a hundred yards or so, we both went full ahead again and made another assault on the river. Again we failed and the same process had to be repeated. Third time, however, proved lucky, and with a smile of triumph we noted that the trees on the river bank were slowly moving astern. The Rhône, I learned, had fallen as much as $1\frac{1}{2}$ metres in the past week, due to absence of rains. This had caused an embarrassing shallowness in certain parts, with the result that our propellers were having difficulty in getting a grip on the water. Our commodore said there was not more than about 5 ft 6 in. of water at this spot, dangerously close to the point where Rhône navigation has to be suspended. Madame said she distinctly heard the bottom several times. We ourselves did not touch.

After lunch and the passage of the confluence of the River Isère at Km. 99, conditions improved a lot and we made progress at the rate of at least $5\frac{1}{2}$ k.p.h., which we thought was pretty good. Soon after six o'clock we made fast to some trees alongside. A ladder was put ashore, but there seemed no point in leaving the boat, as we were at a deserted place near Km. 78. Fortunately, Madame was able to supply us with some bread and milk, for which she refused all payment.

We rose in good heart next morning, for we expected to cover the remaining 78 kilometres to Lyon that day, but our old enemy, the fog, was with us and we could not get away until 0740. Although progress was good, it was soon plain that we would not get to Lyon that night, although at Givors (Km. 34) we slipped our tow and raced on at a good 8 k.p.h. We spent the night at Grigny, a charming little place at Km. 14.

It was a relief next morning to get under way at 0645, without any tow except ourselves, and by 0900 we had covered the 14 kilometres to the lock at La Mulatière. Here there was a sad leave-taking from the ship's company of *C.N.R.3*, with many expressions of mutual esteem. I visited the offices of the Engineer-in-Chief at the lock and duly picked up my 'Autorisation de Circuler' which had been arranged for me in Arles. There was nothing to pay on this and I was told it would take me as far as Bourogne, a small place on the Rhône-Rhine Canal. There I would have to pick up another. We also watered, price Frs 50. I noted that the flow of water over the weir from the River Saône into the Rhône was very heavy and was told that, in view of the lack of water in the Rhône, the Saône waters were being let in to a greater extent than usual.

When we arrived at our berth in Lyon, close to the Tilsitt Bridge in the Saône, I almost went aground, as the river level had fallen so greatly. This is in any case a rotten berth, the Lyon authorities having taken no trouble at all to remove the rocks and boulders that litter the banks. We made fast alongside a pleasure steamer that was fortunately out of commission. There was a German yacht there, too, on her way to the Mediterranean.

It was October 23 and we had left Arles on October 18, so that we had had a very slow passage. This had to be blamed almost entirely on the fog, although engine troubles had also played a small part. We had actually been under way for 57 hours and I was well able to believe the 'mariniers' ' assurances that in summer, when one can navigate from 0400 to 2200 right through, one can expect to get from Arles to Lyon in 3 or 4 days, depending, of course, on the size of tow.

I had had to use my motors for 4 hours 40 minutes in all, which was not bad, especially as I had been warned that I might have to keep them going for many hours each day.

We at once started to find out all we could about how best to get up the River Saône and thence into the Rhône-Rhine Canal. The local branch of the Touring Club de France was friendly, but all they could produce were two maps we already had—namely, the 'Carte des Canaux de France et de Belgique', published by Gerard et Buci, and the equally well-known 'Carte de la Saône de Lyon à St Jean-de-Losne'. The whole of the Rhône-Rhine Canal was therefore still undiscovered territory to us.

Our next call was at the offices of the Ponts et Chaussées, for the Lyon

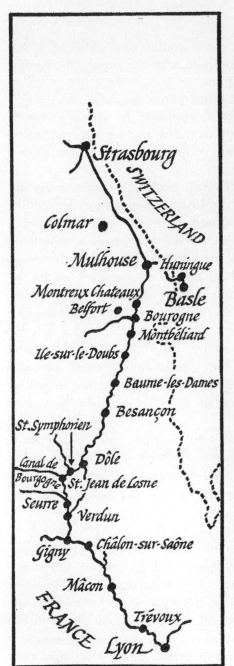

agency of this State organization is responsible for most of the canal. Here we were able to obtain an excellent map of the French canals, published by the French Government, and purporting to show every lock in detail. The map covers the whole of France and is rather expensive, but after some discussion the official allowed us to buy a quarter section of it which showed all the waterways from Lyon to the Rhine. We asked why this excellent publication was not on sale on bookstalls, and were told that it was not for sale to the public as a general rule.

At the Ponts et Chaussées office we were also shown a first-class publication of the French Government called *Guide Officiel de la Navigation Intérieure*, which is an official guide to all the waterways of France and is the best thing of its kind I have ever seen. This edition was, we noted, last revised in 1933. We were told that a revised edition was in preparation. I was unable to beg, borrow or steal the office copy of this work, but by paying Frs 500 to a typist, I was able to get her to type out for me a selection of the pages dealing with the Rhône-Rhine Canal and so have some sort of a guide on which to plan.

Thus armed, and with the laundry

3. From Rhône to Rhine via River Saône and Rhône-Rhine Canal

done, we sailed up the Saône out of Lyon at midday on October 24. It was
a lovely sunny afternoon and we felt relieved, after the tow up the Rhône,
to be sailing under our own power again.

We were navigating solely on the folding map of the Saône, with which
I had successfully negotiated the river downstream the previous year. It
seemed unnecessary to take a pilot, although it was clear from the water-
levels at Lyon that the river was a good couple of feet lower than when I
had last been in it.

All went well until we were past Couzin Lock, some seven miles upstream, where we touched bottom off the Ile de la Condamine. Mercifully,
it was mud, and we were able to get off under our own power. The folding
map, though doubtless excellent of its kind, is often inaccurate and does not
show the channel to be followed in proper detail. It was therefore no
surprise to us when, a few minutes later, we found ourselves fast on the
edge of one of the dykes built to retain the river in the central channel.
This time, no amount of effort could dislodge us. A helpful fisherman took
our C.Q.R. anchor and dropped it for us some way distant and we hauled
on it, but it was no good. Eventually, a barge called the *Sirocco* arrived and
pulled us off with his steel cable. He refused any payment and was
extremely helpful at the next lock, when we had an opportunity of talking
further with him. During the afternoon the British yacht *Fiducia* passed us
southbound.

We had meant to spend the night at Villefranche, but it was rapidly
becoming darker and, chastened by our experiences of the afternoon, we
prudently decided to call a halt and spend the night at Trévoux, a delightful little town with good berths on the left bank by the bridge, which we
reached at 1745.

My log describes the following one as 'a full day'. We slipped from
Trévoux at 0900, as soon as the fog had cleared, but some 8 miles later
on we again had the humiliation of finding ourselves aground. There was
absolutely nothing this time to indicate where the channel was. We were,
in fact, in the middle of what any normal person would have called the
fairway. Again it was impossible to get off, but to our great relief our old
friend the barge *Sirocco* soon turned up astern and, amid gales of laughter
and gratitude, we were once again dragged into safety. This experience

convinced me that, at least in times of low water, it is best to take a pilot in the Saône.

In humble mood, we decided to follow *Sirocco*, although we would not be going so fast as hitherto. Soon, however, we were both overtaken by another Saône barge, the *Aulère*, light, and bound for Châlon-sur-Saône at a rate of knots. Waving good-byes to *Sirocco*, we got into *Aulère's* wake and opened out the throttles. We had some difficulty in keeping up with our new friends and had to concentrate very hard on the steering, as she frequently altered course, following the winding fairway. It was rather cold, pouring with rain and hardly a pleasure trip. But I am convinced that it got us through some bits of river that looked to me highly dangerous, and our gratitude was boundless.

At 1740 we entered Gigny Lock, the last before Châlon-sur-Saône and *Aulère's* skipper announced that he would be spending the night there. This was such an evident disappointment to us that that good fellow thereupon decided to push on.

We thus had the rather hair-raising experience of charging up the river in pitch darkness, trying the while to make out the shadowy shape of our pilot a cable ahead of us. He was burning no navigation lights and the only indication of his presence that we sometimes had was an occasional spark from his exhaust. We were very thankful to arrive at Châlon, where we made fast alongside the Quai Gambetta in the centre of the town. Thanks to our pilots, we had managed to do 62 sea-miles in the Saône that day, including the passage of two locks.

After the rigours of the previous evening, we did not leave Châlon until 1030. It was a lovely, sunny day and we found the Saône in its upper reaches to be far more navigable than in its lower. Although we had no barges to follow, we proceeded at full speed, using intelligent guesses as to where the main channel was likely to be. Some $2\frac{1}{2}$ hours later we passed through the big new lock at Verdun-sur-le-Doubs: this is easily the biggest lock on the Saône, the others all being of moderate size. All are properly manned and one does not have to do anything oneself. The river was looking its best and we were especially attracted by the little township of Seurre, 24 miles upriver from Châlon. There were no groundings or other disasters this day, and we reached St Jean-de-Losne about seven in the evening, making fast with the aid of our searchlight close to the bridge.

We had used our main engines so much in reverse at high speeds trying to get off the mudbanks that the clutches were found to be slipping in reverse. This defect was attended to very cheaply and efficiently by a local mechanic, M. Panout, at St Jean-de-Losne, where we also learned quite a lot about the Rhône-Rhine Canal and other matters which you cannot read about in any book.

Despite the excellence of the French official guide to the waterways, there was, curiously, no mention of the fact that much of the Rhône-Rhine Canal is simply a canalization of the River Doubs. We were shocked to learn from the 'mariniers' of St Jean that, at least from Dôle onwards, we would be foolish not to engage a River Doubs pilot. The river, they said, was full of dangers and we must please ourselves, but in their opinion we had no choice.

St Jean-de-Losne was a miserable little place, noteworthy only for the emergence of the Canal de Bourgogne into the River Saône. This animated the place a little towards evening as the barges arrived to spend the night, but otherwise it was dead.

We slipped next day at 0820 and arrived 20 minutes later at St Symphorien, a hamlet even smaller than St Jean-de-Losne, where the Rhône-Rhine Canal begins. There was an interminable wait while two barges locked through ahead of us; so we had plenty of time to reflect on the new canal we were about to explore.

As long ago as the sixteenth century the French were planning the construction of a canal to link the Rhône to the Rhine via the Saône. But it was not until the middle of the eighteenth century that any concrete plans were drawn up. In 1792 the National Assembly passed a resolution for the building of the 'Canal de l'Est', as it was then to be called. The work did not actually start until the time of the First Empire, by which time the canal was known as the 'Canal Napoleon'. Under Louis XVIII, the canal was rechristened the 'Canal Monsieur' and an Alsatian company called the 'Compagnie du Canal Monsieur' was formed to acquire the finance to realize the project, especially for the last stretch to be cut, that from Montbéliard to Strasbourg.

On December 3, 1832, the first vessel reached Strasbourg from St Jean-de-Losne and the canal thenceforth was known by its present name of 'Rhône-Rhine Canal'. Only small barges—up to 180 tons—could at first navigate it, but in the nineteenth century the canal was enlarged to take vessels of up to 300 tons, although the centre portion between Besançon and the Vosges remained limited until the restoration of Alsace to France in 1918 again gave the French the incentive to enlarge this part.

Originally, the canal ran direct through Besançon, Montbéliard and Mulhouse to Strasbourg, but it was later found that the stretch near Strasbourg ran through such porous ground that it became necessary to aliment it with Rhine water. To this end the branch canal from Huningue (near Basle) to Mulhouse was completed in 1928 and became at the same time an important artery of traffic.

One is constantly reminded of the age of the canal by the inscriptions and dates on the lock walls. Most of these are from the nineteenth century, though some go back as far as the eighteenth. There are also some very recent German ones, dating from the last war, and carrying the name of the 'Organization Todt', which was responsible for work done.

The first few locks of the canal involved a wait of $1\frac{1}{2}$ hours at each while the barges preceding us locked through, but there soon followed a lock-free stretch in which we were able to overtake them, and progress thereafter quickened. It was pouring with rain and the waters were a muddy yellow. The first lock was numbered as No. 75 and by the time we arrived at Dôle that evening we had passed Lock No. 67, having covered 12 miles, of which 10 were in the canal.

Dôle is a charming little town, the birthplace of Pasteur and boasting an interesting large church. I was in two minds whether to engage a pilot for the morrow, when we were due to enter the redoubtable River Doubs. We felt irritated that we had not been made aware of this sooner. There was no mention of a river in the *Guide Officiel de la Navigation Intérieure*, nor in Messrs Imray, Laurie, Norie and Wilson's publication *Inland Waterways of France*. Nor even had the Ponts et Chaussées officials at Lyon made any mention of it. Local opinion varied considerably as to whether or not we should get by without a pilot, but on the whole it seemed to lean to the view that as far as Besançon we should be all right.

And so we sailed from Dôle, leaving early to get a good place in the barge queue, and some 2 miles later, at Lock 65 (Baverans) we entered the River Doubs for the first time. Thereafter all the way to Besançon we found ourselves principally in the river, with short stretches of canal interspersed.

We had been told that if we kept to the towpath side of the river and remained approximately 17 metres distant from the centre of the towpath throughout, we were not likely to run into any trouble, and this we did religiously. We were helped to some extent by the knowledge that, due to the recent rains, the river was pretty full of water.

The passage was not easy, as we had to concentrate so hard and were all the time (at least in the river) on tenterhooks. The speed of the current was an average of 2–3 knots and one of the great difficulties was to be sure of spotting the locks leading out of the river into the canal stretches, as these were generally very small and hidden in foliage. If you happened to enter one at the same moment as a barge came out, you had to wait out in midstream, subject to the vagaries of the currents. The locks are always kept open for downcoming traffic, as this is unable to stop and wait (due to the current), whereas upgoing traffic can breast the stream while biding its time to enter. This means that you have to wait at every lock while the gates are opened. The river and mountain scenery was perfectly beautiful. After $11\frac{1}{2}$ hours under way, having negotiated twenty-three locks, of which four were open (serving the purpose of floodgates), we arrived exhausted at Besançon and moored in the basin to the south of the Citadel just before the canal tunnel. It was still raining hard.

Touristically, Besançon is a 'must' and we spent a pleasant day of rest there though we were anxious about the continuing rain. Reggie Paul, my second crewman, left us here to go back to England, and I asked the excellent chief lock-keeper whether he knew of anyone with local knowledge who would care for a canal trip as far as Basle. To our gratification, he produced a young fellow called Jean Seger, son of the principal Doubs pilot, and we sailed next morning up the swollen river with Jean at the helm. We hoped to make Ile-sur-le-Doubs that day. This was 33 miles upriver and there were twenty-eight intervening locks, but it could be done. We charged along at full revs, Jean at the wheel in the river and Jim or I taking over in the short canal stretches, but when we arrived at Baume-les-Dames at lunch-time (having covered 16 miles and passed twelve locks) we found the floodgates closed. No amount of pleading would persuade the lock-keeper to open them, and we were thus forced to bite our nails in the canal and hope it would stop raining.

The flood gauge on the lock showed 2 m. 70 and we were told it would have to drop at least 10 centimetres before the gates could be opened. The floodgates were due for replacement on November 15 by a new lock, which could be opened and closed at any state of the river, so we were doubly unlucky to have arrived there a fortnight earlier.

But on the morning of November 1—2 days later—the water-level had fallen to 2 m. 57; the gates were opened and on we went. The river was still in flood and we estimated the current at 7–8 knots in parts, so that progress was slow. At many of the lock gates, the combination of current and flood water pouring out of the lock sluices made it hopeless to approach to put a man ashore to help in locking and we simply had to wait. Most of the locks had one man or one woman only in attendance, so that we always had to give a hand—and gladly—ourselves.

We arrived at Ile-sur-le-Doubs for a late lunch and realized that we were at last rid of this tiresome if beautiful river. Snow lay thick on the surrounding Jura and we were well over 750 ft above sea-level. At Ile-sur-le-Doubs we took aboard some of the new pink-tinted diesel oil, price Frs 18.90 per litre, and felt much happier. After lunch we pressed on and spent the night at the small industrial town of Colombier-Fontaines. We had reached Lock No. 21, having passed twenty-two locks that day and covered 23 miles. Locks Nos. 34 to 36 were the worst I had ever had to negotiate.

The 2nd of November was notable chiefly for our reaching the summit level of the canal and starting to descend—always a much pleasanter process. We slipped early from Colombier-Fontaines and arrived at Montbéliard by 1015. Here we stopped for some shopping and to see the town, which was pleasant enough, though not worthy of a lengthy visit. It is in this region that the canal passes through the famous 'Belfort gap' between the Jura and the Vosges. We also caught sight of the Peugeot motor works, much of them still in construction. It is planned later that there shall be an extensive inland port here. Several of the locks were entirely unattended and we had to do all the work ourselves. In some cases this was due to the incidence of the sacred lunch-hour and in others to the keeper being engaged on work elsewhere.

The average pay of a lock-keeper on this canal was Frs 35,000 a month, which was not reckoned to be very high. It thus often happened that the man took on other work as well, leaving his wife to tend the gates. Most of the ladies concerned seemed to be pretty stoutly built, which was perhaps just as well. As we approached the summit level between Montreux Château (Lock No. 3 south) and Valdieu (Lock No. 2 north), I observed that our barometer had fallen to 28.65, the lowest reading it has ever recorded. We were here at a level of 341 metres above the sea, well over 1,000 ft high.

The summit level of this canal is fairly lengthy, Locks Nos. 1 and 2 south and Lock No. 1 north having been suppressed as no longer necessary. The level is fed by the water from a lake on the left-hand side going north, which in turn derives its water from another lake near Belfort. Shortly before reaching the summit level we had passed a branch of the canal lead-ing to Belfort itself. This branch is known as the Canal de Montbéliard à la Haute Saône and is 18 kilometres long.

At this point I suddenly remembered that, according to our maps, we had passed the Bourogne canal offices some five locks previously and at once started to make inquiries about handing in my existing 'Autorisation de Circuler'. At Lyon, I had been told to exchange it at Bourogne for another, which would get me as far as the Rhine. Quite a lot of telephoning ensued, the upshot of which was the information that the office at Bourogne had been suppressed some years previously. In the circumstances, I was advised to continue with my existing piece of paper, which in any case no one ever seemed to bother to read.

On leaving the summit level we at once entered the famous set of locks known as the 'Valdieu series'. There are eighteen of these almost on top of each other, and one man has four or five under his care. As light was failing, we could not manage to get the whole way through them and spend the night at Dannemarie, as we had hoped, and by half past five we found that the lock-keepers were refusing to go on working. We had, however, managed to pass through nine of them before settling down to a quiet night in the midst of the French countryside. We had that day negotiated as many as twenty-six locks and, now that all were of a descending kind, we felt that we had really broken the back of this arduous canal trip.

Next day we were determined to make Mulhouse, so we started at 0800 and made excellent progress, our average time in each lock being as little as five minutes from entry to leaving it. There was, furthermore, very little

1. The m.y. *Dame des Iles* 23 T.M. measurement 48 ft long 11 ft beam, 4 ft 5 in draught.

2. The author's 54 ft Silver-built m.y. *September Tide*.

3. Joseph Pariset, our Rhône pilot, and indeed to many yachts.

4. Marseille. The 'Vieux Port' showing yacht moorings. (*French Govt. Tourist Office.*)

5. *Dame des Iles* in tow by *C.N.R.*3 Rhône. John Marriner on the right.

6. The famous St Benozet Bridge at Avignon taken from on board. Note the run of the current, probably 4/5 knots.

7. *Dame des Iles* at her berth in Basel, alongside the Hotel des Trois Rois.

8. About to lock through at Kembs soon after leaving Basel downstream.

traffic, so that we were even able to stop for lunch before arriving at Mulhouse at 1530.

There is a drop of 80 metres (about 250 ft) between the summit level and Mulhouse, a distance by canal of about 40 kilometres, so one can appreciate that each of the forty locks negotiated is necessary to bring one downhill such a distance. We made fast in Mulhouse opposite the main railway station, which is the best berth for a yacht. If we had gone on further, we should have entered a very dirty part of the town basin. The town, once Swiss, has the spaciousness of a German city. It did not seem at all French to me, reminding me very much of some of the Black Forest towns.

Next day, November 4, was perhaps the most momentous in our trip, for we planned to arrive in Switzerland, surely not a very ordinary destination for a yacht. We passed through the last lock in the Rhône-Rhine Canal proper, Lock No. 41 in the fall towards the Rhine, and soon afterwards, at a curious sort of roundabout called Ile Napoléon, branched off to the right into the Canal de Huningue leading to Switzerland. We could, of course, have continued in the Rhône-Rhine Canal towards Strasbourg, but the journey to Switzerland and thence down the Rhine seemed infinitely more interesting.

The journey along the straight, broad and almost lockless Canal de Huningue went very quickly. It was broader than the Rhône-Rhine Canal and an electric towing tram ran alongside it. There were four locks in all its 28 kilometres length—at Hombourg, Kembs and two smaller places— and the rise was in each case very small. We finally reached Huninguc at 1500 and made fast in the midst of a flock of barges of all nationalities. I went ashore to find out how to lock through the very imposing locks into the Rhine and realized to my dismay that, since it was a Sunday, the lock did not operate due to the absence of Customs men from duty.

The prospect of spending a wet Sunday evening in this dreary marine no-man's-land was so appalling that I went on foot for the 2 or 3 kilometres that separated the lock from the road frontier H.Q. and routed out the chief Customs officer, an obliging Alsatian called Mueller, and got him to issue me with a special permit to lock through on a Sunday.

At 1710 we throbbed out into the swift-flowing Rhine. Last light was already upon us. It was a curious sensation, after so long in a canal, to be belting hell for leather against the Rhine current. We were making for the 'Mittlere Rheinbrücke', a bridge in the centre of the city of Basle.

As we approached it in the gloom, however, there seemed to be some small craft made fast there, so we decided to make for the opposite side of the river. Shining our searchlight on likely moorings, we had the unpleasant experience of going aground on some rocks. The boat heeled over dangerously as the current caught her and I thought for a moment we might have to abandon ship, but Jim had the presence of mind to go full astern and we shook ourselves free, afterwards making fast at the Mittlere Rheinbrücke quay, in a 5–6 knot current. We were thankful to arrive.

There were several willing hands to take our warps, and the moment we were made fast a delegate from the Basler Segel Klub (Basle Sailing Club) came aboard and bade us welcome. Monsieur André Baschong, the commodore of the club, and some friends, visited us next day and did everything possible to help us.

Only one untoward incident occurred. On the evening of our arrival, I thought it would be nice to take Jim and young Jean, our Alsatian pilot, who would be leaving us next day, out to dinner ashore. We visited a restaurant called the Baslerstab, the equivalent, so I was told, of one of the better-class Maison Lyons. We were just finishing dinner, when we were asked to step outside into the kitchen. Here we found a row of police. We were suspected of having stolen some money from the cloakroom, the pilot while he was visiting the lavatory and I while I was doing some telephoning. A lachrymose lady was in attendance, apparently the victim of the loss. It was not long before the Swiss realized their mistake. Although no apology was made to us, we thought it best not to make too much of the incident, though we were inwardly boiling with rage at such an inhospitable reception in a country which so often advertises its hospitality. It was a warning to us for the future—at least in the *petit-bourgeois* atmosphere of Switzerland—not to go ashore unless we were more respectably dressed.

Next morning we were visited by a helpful Customs official, who explained that we should have cleared Customs, on entering Swiss waters, at the Customs Office at Klein-Hueningen, opposite where we had emerged from the canal. The French, when they took our Customs *laissez-passer* from us on leaving France, had not been able to tell us where to go.

However, the matter was solved by my taking the tram to the Customs office and securing clearance.

The next thing to do was to find out all we could about how to get down the Rhine. There is no official information published on how to do this, since the commercial traffic knows all about it and yachts are rarely seen. The Customs suggested we should try the Schweizerische Reederei, A.G., the biggest Swiss Rhine-shipping concern. Here we had the pleasure of meeting, and subsequently being visited by, a Herr Merz, who was a mine of information and help. He made us a present of one of the few copies in existence of a Rhine map from Basle to the sea, showing its course kilometre by kilometre. This proved of the very greatest assistance. He also gave us a list of his company's offices and agents at every main centre and promised us their help in all matters, including the arrangement of pilotage where required.

Being new boys, we were still in total ignorance of where pilots would be necessary and how much of the Rhine was canalized. We learned that the river was in course of canalization over a long period from Basle to Strasbourg, but that to date the canal only extended from a few kilometres south of Basle to the locks at Fessenheim, 35 kilometres below. This immense work, known as the Grand Canal d'Alsace, is still under construction, and serves not only as a great aid to navigation but also as a vital source of hydroelectric power to France, through whose territory it runs.

This stretch of canal, indeed, the whole of the Rhine, is a shining example of how international problems can cease to exist when goodwill replaces distrust. Not once the whole way from Basle to the German frontier were we obstructed or even questioned, although our way lay through three countries and all around us were river craft of Swiss, French, German, Netherlands and Belgian flags, many of them carrying mixed crews. Even money was freely interchangeable.

On November 7 we finally left Basle, sailing at 1135, some while after we had intended, but we had to wait for the fog to lift. Five or six kilometres below Basle we entered the Grand Canal d'Alsace and were able to increase speed. The huge locks at Kembs were quickly negotiated and we carried on at full speed down the broad and sunlit canal towards the next locks, those of Ottmarsheim, some 14 kilometres farther.

In the canal we had our first taste of Rhine traffic and its signal system.

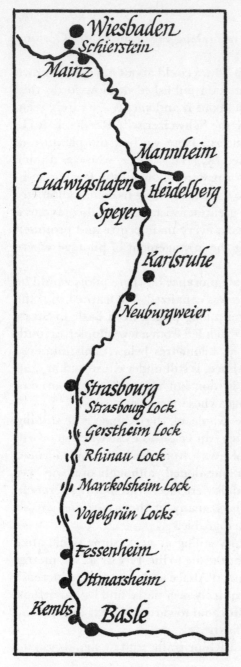

There are not many signals which it is essential to know, but these must be carefully observed and implicitly obeyed, otherwise you will get into serious trouble and may be faced with a large insurance claim.

They are as follows:

1. Ascending traffic determines the course to be followed by descending. An ascending craft displays a large blue flag on that side of her on which she wishes the descending craft to pass. This is far the most important signal to look out for.

2. A yellow cylinder at a vessel's masthead indicates that she is towing.

3. A yellow disc displayed by a vessel indicates that she is the last in a convoy. Convoys may be as much as six or seven vessels in length, excluding their tug.

4. A blue flag displayed at a vessel's masthead means that she wishes to overtake that immediately ahead of her.

5. In connection with (4) above, vessels overtaking must leave those overtaken to starboard.

6. Flags worn at half-mast mean that the vessel concerned is not under way.

7. A white flag means the vessel showing it wishes to pass through the lock she is approaching.

4. The Rhine

8. A red flag indicates danger. It may mean that the route shown is barred to navigation.

9. Red and white flags mean 'Approach with caution'.

10. A green flag, generally worn below the ship's ensign, means that she has cleared Customs and is carrying a transit cargo.

N.B.—Relative to (1) above, an ascending vessel must acknowledge this signal by herself hoisting a blue flag on the side she intends to pass. In the case of yachts, however, this is not essential.

There are also a number of conventional sound signals in use on the Rhine, and it is just as well to recognize them. Here they are:

—	Attention. Always sounded on approaching a lock going upstream.
— —	Sounded on approaching a lock going downstream. Request for a bridge to open.
–	I am altering course to starboard.
– –	I am altering course to port.
– – –	My engines are going hard astern.
– – – –	I am unable to manoeuvre.
– – – – –	You must not overtake me.
— –	I am making a full circle to starboard.
— – –	I am making a full circle to port.
— — –	I wish to overtake you and am altering course to starboard.
— — – –	I wish to overtake you and am altering course to port.
— — —	Prefix to a signal made before entering or leaving harbour.

It is worth trying to memorize, or at least to write down, all of these before attempting the Rhine, which is not an easy river. Continual concentration is necessary to avert a disaster.

We had also made some inquiries in Basle regarding the advisability of taking a pilot anywhere. Opinion was divided, but on the whole people agreed that, although for a yacht there was no compulsory pilotage at any point, it would be wise to take one aboard at the following stretches:

A. Fessenheim Locks to Strasbourg. Fee: S.frs 35, with S.frs 2 per hour for every hour's wait after the first 2 hours, in the event of the vessel being delayed sailing. Pilots are also apt to ask for journey money, but this should be resisted.

B. Strasbourg to Ludwigshafen Mannheim. A German pilot's standard fee is DM. 42.50, with no journey money. He is entitled to DM. 2 for every hour's delay in starting after the first 2 hours.

A French pilot's standard fee is F.frs 2,205, with F.frs 1,000 of journey money. He is entitled to F.frs 120 for every hour's delay in starting after the first 2 hours.

C. Bingen to St Goar. Standard fee DM. 20, composed of DM. 12 for the Bingen–Kaub stretch and DM. 8 for Kaub–St Goar.

It was felt that we could manage to get from Mannheim to Bingen without a pilot, as the run of current in that stretch was very much less.

I had, of course, made inquiries about my own capacity to take a vessel down this crowded highway. The answer was that, where the vessel concerned was of less than 15 tons net, no 'driving licence' was necessary. This qualification we mercifully fulfilled.

The depths of water vary in the Rhine according to the season. On the day we left Basle there was at least a depth of 2.30 metres between Strasbourg and Mannheim and about 2 metres between Basle and Strasbourg. The following are the normal minimum depths in the various stretches:

Basle to Strasbourg	1.20 m. (4 ft)
Strasbourg to Karlsruhe	1.50 m. (5 ft)
Karlsruhe to St Goar	1.70 m. ($5\frac{1}{2}$ ft)
St Goar to Cologne	2.10 m. (7 ft)
Cologne to Duisburg-Ruhrort	1.80 m. (6 ft)
Duisburg-Ruhrort to the sea	2.20 m. ($7\frac{1}{4}$ ft)

Generally speaking, in the upper reaches of the river, low water prevails in January and February, and high water in June and July, when the thaw is on in the Alps. On the Middle Rhine, from Bingen to Bonn, the highest water-level accompanies the spring floods in March. The level of the river at the various points of measurement is taken daily at 0500 and the levels broadcast, so that it is easy to check.

The whole of the river is marked with kilometre and half-kilometre signs, so that it is easy to determine exactly where one is if one possesses a river chart. These are, unfortunately, out of print now. I am willing to lend my copy to any yachtsman proposing to make the trip.

Since the war Swiss shipping on the river has developed very considerably and Switzerland is the nation which, in my opinion, has developed the most reliable network of agencies throughout the length of the river. It seems logical, therefore, to deal with the main Swiss Rhine-shipping Company, the Schweizerische Reederei, A.G., if one wants a good liaison for the trip, especially as the staff are courteous and efficient. I therefore give below a list of the company's agencies at the principal ports likely to be touched:

BASLE

Schweizerische Reederei A.G., Rittergasse, 20. Tel. 24-98-98, or 22-30-02. Herr Merz.

STRASBOURG (PORT DU RHIN)

Compagnie Suisse de Navigation, S.A., 5 Rue Dunkerque. Tel. 35-08-81. M. Grieder.

MANNHEIM-LUDWIGSHAFEN

Alpina Rheinkontor, G.m.b.H., Parkstrasse, 70. Tel. 6-35-36. Herr Muessig.

DUISBURG-RUHRORT

Alpina Schiffahrt und Spedition G.m.b.H., Dammstrasse, 7. Tel. 4-08-57. Herr P. Thommen.

ROTTERDAM

N. V. Alpina Scheepvaart Mij., Rivierstraat, 9-11. Tel. 2-51-60. M. J. de Klerk.

It did not take us very long to get to the lock at Ottmarsheim and to lock through, although there was a lengthy wait before we could enter, due to some traffic locking through in the opposite direction.

On arrival at Fessenheim Locks about 1630 we went alongside the Rhine pilots' accommodation barge, at which the Swiss shipping company had arranged we should call, and discovered that our pilot was waiting for us at the lock.

There was unfortunately some argument with this gentleman after he had boarded us, bicycle and all. He claimed that, in addition to the agreed pilotage fee, we should pay him an extra DM. 20 for his journey money. As there had been no mention of this in our agreement with our friends in Basle, I quickly put him ashore and bade him farewell. We managed to book another and more reasonably inclined pilot to board us next morning.

When, however, morning came, we found ourselves shrouded in thick fog and were unable to leave our berth all day. So we spent the day chatting to the various bargee families and walking rather miserably through the fog to the local canteen. For there was no village at Fessenheim. All that existed was an impromptu series of barrack-like huts housing the workers on the canal project. Fessenheim Locks themselves were brandnew, only having been opened to traffic about a month before our arrival. Since we made this trip the Vogelgruen, Marckolsheim, Rhinau and Gerstheim Locks on the Grand Canal d'Alsace below Fessenheim have all been opened to traffic. The last projected lock, that of Strasbourg itself, is due for completion at the end of 1967.

At length we were able to leave. As we swept out of the lock approach channel into the turbulent Rhine waters next morning I was very glad we had taken a pilot. It was a lovely day and, freed from the responsibility of taking the wheel, we were able to admire the scenery and relax. The Rhine here forms the frontier between France and Germany and the numerous blown-up pill-boxes on the German side were a reminder of 'Die Wacht am Rhein'. With a 3–4 knot current to help us, we covered the 80-odd kilometres to Strasbourg in exactly 4 hours, an average speed over the ground of 12½ knots. Emile, our good Alsatian pilot, had had a hard time of it following the winding channel.

Strasbourg harbour is not a nice place for a yacht, and is far from the centre of the town. We arranged to fill our tanks next morning with dutyfree diesel oil at the usual French prices from the Antar Company's installation.

The German pilot that the Swiss had laid on for me duly arrived at 0800. He was a pleasant and serious young man named Heinrich Haesacker, and there was no argument about fees. He at first wanted us to wear a blue answering flag, but finally abandoned the idea as unnecessary.

At midday we were given ocular proof of the desirability of pilotage when we sighted the Swiss barge *Sittertal* hard and fast aground on a mudbank at Km. 350. Four kilometres later we entered the small German Customs harbour at Neuburgweier and the German Customs came aboard for their inspection. They were extremely reasonable and the formalities were quickly over. The current runs fast at this particular point and turning around and making the harbour mouth was quite an adventure. The barges are, of course, examined at anchor in the stream.

And so on, through Speyer—past its famous cathedral and under its great new bridge, until we made fast at Mannheim soon after 1600. Here the stream ran much less fast, so that turning into it was an easy matter.

There is little of interest in Mannheim, but Heidelberg is only 20 minutes distant by fast electric tram, so that we were able to visit this delightful city. We had thought of going to it up the River Neckar, but realized that this would have been rather a waste of time.

The Swiss at Mannheim advised me, after all, to take a pilot down to Wiesbaden. Owing to various unforeseen river disasters, the volume of traffic was very great at the time and they thought it would be wiser to take pilotage. On inquiry, however, at the pilots' offices alongside, I found that the fee was about DM. 35, which I thought a bit high.

So, as soon as we had raised our masts—there being now no more bridges with a less headroom than 8.96 m. at highest water—we slipped pilotless downstream. We had not gone very far before a police boat halted us and we were compelled to make fast alongside a barge and wait an hour or so. Apparently, some cable-laying had been going on across the river and traffic was temporarily held up.

We were checked several times by police boats on our way downstream past the places with the romantic names from the wine list—Nierstein, Germersheim and so on. We had thought of spending the night in the Customs Harbour at Mainz, but when we got there it seemed such a miserable place that we decided to push on, and at 1615 we made fast in the very pleasant little harbour of Wiesbaden-Schierstein, where we found a flotilla of United States fast patrol launches. Schierstein is a protected harbour and is only 15 minutes from the centre of Wiesbaden by motor-bus I can recommend it as a good place to lie.

Since leaving Basle, we had come 178 miles down the Rhine at an average speed of about 11 knots over the ground.

We sailed from Wiesbaden-Schierstein harbour at midday. We could see that there was a lot of Rhine shipping at anchor in the stream off the harbour mouth. This was due to the congestion caused by a recent incident at the notorious narrows off Bingen, known as the 'Binger Loch'. Fog had descended suddenly one evening and a number of vessels had sunk or come

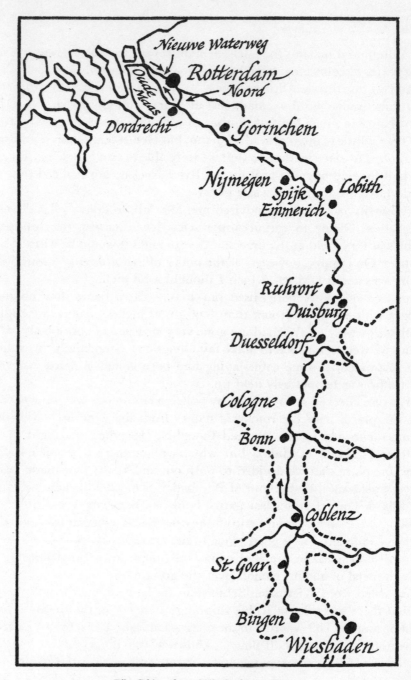

5. *The Rhine from Wiesbaden to Rotterdam*

into collision with each other. The passage had been blocked to shipping for some days and was even now navigable only with difficulty. The result had been a tremendous congestion, some of which we had already noted farther upstream. Barges were authorized to move only when allowed by the river police, who were having no easy job of it.

We crept downstream, there being little current here, past the waiting barges, but 6 miles farther down we were hailed by a police launch and thought it prudent to stop. We accordingly went alongside a waiting barge for an hour. It is often very difficult, even with a good knowledge of German, to make out what it is that the police launches are trying to tell you. Their skippers often speak a kind of river dialect and they have no proper loud-hailers. Furthermore, they are inclined to rush off without having made sure you have understood.

The crew of the barge we were lying against advised us to carry on downstream. So we did, meaning to arrive at Bingen and arrange for a pilot next morning. It is absolutely essential to take pilotage between Bingen and St Goar, due to the narrow passages and swift current.

On our way, we passed the cause of part of the trouble, a couple of grounded barges that a group of tugs was busily trying to dislodge.

The Swiss shipping company was not represented at Bingen, but it was an easy matter to arrange for a pilot, their headquarters being just alongside. I bought several gallons of excellent red wine for our container, and learned afterwards that it was Greek!

It was most disappointing that next morning was misty and dark, for we were due to pass through some of the loveliest river scenery in Europe. Our pilot, Jakob Kauper, boarded us sharp at 0700, and after a light breakfast we swung out into midstream and awaited the police launch which was to tell us when we could sail. Soon after 0900 we got the O.K. and hurtled off through the rapids past the Mäuseturm signal station in midstream.

It is perhaps as well at this stage to list the signals which are given on this dangerous section of river, though with a pilot to watch out for them much of the responsibility is taken over:

Signals Shown from the Mäuseturm at Bingen

(Binger Loch channel to the right and New Channel to the left, looking downstream)

1. White disc on right yardarm = Convoy may descend New Channel.
2. Orange disc on left yardarm = A single vessel may descend New Channel.
3. Orange disc on left and white disc on right yardarm = A raft may descend the New Channel.
4. White flag on right yardarm = A convoy may descend the Binger Loch.
5. Orange flag on left yardarm = A single vessel may descend the Binger Loch.
6. Orange flag on left and white flag on right yardarm = A raft may descend the Binger Loch.
7. Red-and-white disc on lower flagstaff = Ascending traffic must stop at entrance to New Channel.
8. Red-and-white flag on lower flagstaff = Ascending traffic must halt at entry to Binger Loch.
9. Red-and-white disc and red-and-white flag on lower flagstaff = All ascending traffic must stop at entry to either channel.
10. Red-and-white disc at mainmast peak = No traffic allowed through New Channel.
11. Red-and-white rectangle at mainmast peak = No traffic allowed through Binger Loch.
12. Red-and-white disc and red-and-white rectangle at mainmast peak = No traffic allowed through New Channel or through Binger Loch.

Signals Shown from the Ochsenturm at Oberwesel

1. One white light (seen from downstream) = A convoy is descending.
2. One red light (seen from downstream) = A single vessel is on her way downstream.
3. One red and one white light (seen from downstream) = A raft is on its way downstream.
4. Two red lights (seen from upstream) = Navigation suspended below Oberwesel.
5. One white light (seen from upstream) indicates that the signal station is announcing descending traffic to those waiting below.

So much for the signals used by these two signal stations, which control the traffic for the 20 kilometres that separate them. In addition, there are a number of minor signal stations erected on strategic points at the bends and each of these uses another set of signals to warn traffic of what is going on between Lorch and St Goar. These are:

1. White flag on upper yardarm = A convoy is descending.
2. Red flag on upper yardarm = An independent is descending.
3. Red flag over white flag = A raft is descending.
4. Red flag with vertical white stripe = Navigation is suspended.

We noticed this system working extremely well, the flags superseding each other very rapidly as the traffic situation changed. It is all very confusing for a new-comer, though the system is well known to all river people. I mention it in some detail, less to provide a working guide than to convince intending yachtsmen on this stretch of the necessity for having someone aboard with them who knows what it all means. There are also a number of lesser signals in use on this complicated and important stretch of river. I will not risk boring readers with them now, but if anyone wants them I can supply them.

Pilots on this stretch are not strictly supposed to take vessels farther than Kaub, 17 kilometres below Bingen, where other pilots wait to take the vessels down from there to St Goar, 10 kilometres farther on.

We were aiming at making Cologne before nightfall if possible. Bingen–Cologne is 156 kilometres, so we had to step on it. There was an immense amount of traffic, but the current eased off considerably after St Goar and the map indicated very few dangers, so that we felt justified in proceeding at full throttle. By then we had become used to the complicated system of signalling in use on the river and, although we never dared relax, we felt pretty confident. There must, however, always be two men on the bridge, for it is often difficult to tell at a distance whether a vessel coming upstream is signalling or not. When you think that every vessel carries at least one house-flag, a national ensign, some sort of burgee depending on the whim of the skipper, and very often leaves her blue signalling flags carelessly placed, it is often as well to have a second opinion.

Coblenz, with its fortress and famous Deutscher Eck, was passed soon after midday. Visibility became poor and at one time it looked as though we would be forced to stop, but, just as hopes were at their lowest the mists cleared and we passed Koenigswinter and Bonn in sunshine. Knowing what perils attached to night navigation on the river, I was not a bit anxious to arrive at Cologne after nightfall, but the speed with which the kilometre signs were flying by suggested that our rate of advance was not less than 20 kilometres an hour, so at Bonn we took the decision to press on to Cologne.

Dusk was approaching as we arrived under the Bayenthal Bridge a few kilometres upriver from the city. Some friends had suggested that we halt here, as this was the spot that most of the local yachts preferred. There were indeed a number of yachts and small craft moored alongside the banks, but it was so very far away from the town centre that we decided to carry on. It is all very well to keep one's yacht a few miles from where one lives, but when one is a visitor one prefers to be in the centre of things.

We arrived beneath the Deutz Bridge at 1700 precisely, just as last light was fading and went alongside a river steamer pontoon berth. This was far too lively, however, and a few minutes later we shifted to a point just downstream from the Rhine harbour, on the left bank. Here it was nice and quiet and there were some steps abeam for getting ashore. An official from the harbour master's office arrived and tried his best to persuade us to enter the river harbour, but we managed to get his permission to stay where we were.

While in Cologne, I had to have some repairs to my port engine and these were very quickly and efficiently done for me by the Weber-Schiff concern opposite where we lay. Herr Theodor Weber, whose family have been in the ship-chartering and operating business on the Rhine for some hundreds of years, dating from the time when the first of his line rowed a ferry to and fro across the river, was the soul of kindness and I readily commend his services to any visiting British yachtsman. My bill for two days' work on the engine amounted to the equivalent of £5. I reflected that, had I had the same work done in the South of France it would have come to about four times this amount.

We also fuelled, at a price of DM. 0.16½ per litre, which is roughly the same price as the duty-free French price. In order to get duty-free facilities, I had first to visit the Customs and get a form from them to show the pump-station, which was on a pontoon by the harbour entrance. I also bought some paraffin for our heater, which cost DM. 0.63 per litre, and watered free of charge. The staff at the pontoon were excellent.

There were harbour dues to pay at Cologne, totalling DM. 2—for the four nights of our stay.

The cruise for the short leg downriver from Cologne to Düsseldorf was made in bright sunshine, the 60 kilometres being covered in exactly 3 hours. We were at first not quite sure where the basin used by the Düsseldorfer Yacht Club was located, as our map also mentioned a Sporthafen, which we at first mistook for it, but we soon realized our mistake and carried on for 1 kilometre more until it lay on our starboard beam. Getting in and out of this small harbour is quite a manoeuvre, as the current runs fast past the entrance and one has to choose a moment for turning when traffic permits.

Although it was out of season, the yacht club did its best to help us, and a glance at the visitors' book spoke of many satisfied visiting yachts. The clubhouse was excellent and the arrangement of berths at the pontoons very convenient. As is the case with many yacht clubs, however, it suffered —from the visitors' point of view—from being situated rather a long way from the centre of the town. It might pay a visiting yacht, therefore, to make fast at one of the several quays on the right bank just above the bridge, where she would be alongside all the main centres.

Next day we covered another short leg—from Düsseldorf to Duisburg, a distance of only 32 kilometres, which we accomplished in exactly 2 hours. The current was now very much less. Duisburg, and its associated port of Ruhrort, is the biggest inland port in Europe and dates from the eleventh century, although it was not until 1317 that the Ruhr coalmines were begun. There are a number of basins and canals leading off it, also the River Ruhr here joins the Rhine and gives its name to the great industrial hinterland adjacent. Duisburg from the river is quite a sight; the forests of tall chimneys and furnaces belching smoke into the evening sky and the vast agglomeration of Rhine shipping in the river hardly qualify it as a yachtsman's paradise, but it is nevertheless most impressive and it is far from impossible to find a quiet berth. We ourselves chose to enter the short canal known as the Aussenhafen or Outer Harbour, which is the first turning on the right coming downriver after passing under the overhead cables. We made fast outside the locks leading to the Inner Harbour and spent an

undisturbed night, in preparation for the long stretch planned for the
next day.

The night was very cold indeed, and when we went on deck next morning the warps were frozen solid and there was a sheet of ice inside the
wheelhouse all over the glass windows. This had to be thawed before we
could start. It was windy when we got into the Rhine again and there was
a lot of spray, which splashed over the windows and promptly froze,
making visibility rather tricky. For about 5 miles below Duisburg, the
traffic was intense, but the river gradually broadened out considerably and
the going became much easier.

We arrived at Emmerich, the German frontier control post, at 1400,
which was 4 hours after slipping from Duisburg, and rather sooner than we
had expected. We entered the small Customs harbour and surrendered
the Customs *laissez-passer* which we had been given on entering Germany.
The German Customs men were most reasonable and the formalities were
quickly over, although, in order to secure attention I had had to go ashore
and make myself known at the offices.

A curious formality of this post was that one was given a Customs
clearance receipt, the price for which was DM. 0.70. This had to be
surrendered off Spijk, a village 4 kilometres farther downriver, where a
launch put out and came alongside to collect its tribute. All this was
accomplished without incident.

Five kilometres beyond Spijk, one has to stop at Lobith, which is the
Netherlands frontier control post. We turned into the stream and went
alongside a group of barges that were also being cleared. No one took any
notice of us, so I went ashore and a friendly Dutch Customs man soon
came aboard.

I do not think they can be very used to yachts in these waters, for he was
quite nonplussed by the sight of our stores. We still had about two cases of
gin and whisky and a few thousand cigarettes. At first he said we would
have to pay on the lot, and be refunded on leaving the country for any
unused balance. I produced, however, a certificate written in Dutch issued
by the Royal Thames Yacht Club which asked that we be accorded the
recognized courtesies normally accorded to yachts, and this seemed to have
some effect on him. He went off and returned smilingly in a few minutes to
announce that we could go on our way unhindered, although we would

probably be inspected again before leaving the Netherlands to make sure that we had not consumed more than a reasonable quantity of our stores, a list of which he made out and signed for us. The Dutch naturally have to ensure that yachts are not trading in excisable goods.

It is only fair to say that, in all the years I have yachted to the Netherlands, I have never even once been troubled by their Customs men. It is, however, only reasonable to expect that, on a great commercial river like the Rhine, rather different conditions might be met.

It was then getting too dark to make Nijmegen, the next big town (24 kilometres distant) before nightfall, so we spent a quiet night in the little harbour at Lobith. The town does a thriving trade with passing river-folk, many of whom use it as a sort of postal headquarters. They have the right to certain Customs concessions for small quantities of dutiable goods, provided these are ordered in advance in writing. The local shops are thus piled high with duty-free parcels awaiting collection on the vessel's next passage.

Icing again delayed departure next morning, but we were glad to have both the frontier control posts behind us and thus avoid any further delays of this kind. It was a lovely sunny day and the trip down the broad river—there being now only a negligible current—was most pleasant. One still had to keep a look-out for traffic and its signals, but, although there was a great deal of it, it was much less concentrated.

Not being anxious to lower and raise our masts again, we had decided to make Dordrecht and then pass through the Oude Maas down to the Nieuwe Waterweg and so up to Rotterdam, rather than turn right at Dordrecht into the Noord and arrive at Rotterdam from upriver, thus encountering four or five low fixed bridges on arrival. This situation we checked with a Dutch Army patrol boat shortly before making Dordrecht.

In Dordrecht itself we had to go alongside and wait for the opening of the swinging span of the railway bridge, but only for 15 minutes. From Gorinchem, 20 kilometres above Dordrecht, the river had become tidal and we had planned our trip to take advantage of the falling tide down the Oude Maas, hoping to arrive at the junction with the Nieuwe Waterweg as the tide turned, so taking advantage of the floodstream up to Rotterdam. This plan was carried out in theory, but in practice it was slightly obstructed by the three lifting bridges in the Oude Maas, for two of which we had to wait before passing below. These bridges in theory open on request every 15 minutes.

It was dark as we turned into the great waterway up to Rotterdam and the river was alive with the lights of passing traffic. Fortunately, I had been in the river before, and knew where the harbour was located where we could find the 'De Maas' Yacht Club. In due course, the friendly buildings turned up and we steamed into the quiet little harbour. My first trip down the Rhine was over.

2

Some New Ways South

The Burgundy and Marne routes through France

It was early May 1960 and the Baie de la Seine was a mirror of glass as we sped over it beyond the Havre light-vessel towards Honfleur.

We were bound for the 'Med' again. I was looking forward not only to the lovely cruise up the Seine to Paris but to going south by yet another canal route, that known as 'La Route de Bourgogne', the Burgundy route through the most central and reputedly the most beautiful district of France.

Moreover, I had meanwhile sold my old vessel *Dame des Iles* to some people who had steamed her out to Mombasa and thence shipped her ignominiously to a lake in East Africa, where she chugs gloomily away to this day. With the proceeds and then some I had 'acquired larger tonnage' (as the saying goes) and the yacht whose wheel I had in my hands was a wooden boat by Silvers, 54 ft long, with twin diesels, and drawing 5 ft (a shade more than my old *Dame des Iles*). To conform with my approaching period of life, I had called her *September Tide*. Added to my curiosity as to how my new command would behave in inland waterways, was my interest in seeing to what extent France had changed since my last visit.

Certainly Honfleur had not. The same sleeping tranquillity in the basin, the same easy nonchalance of the lock-keepers and the same nostalgic charm in the buildings of the 'Lieutenance' at the harbour mouth. It was with regret that we took the tide next morning as soon as the lock gates opened (here they open them $2\frac{1}{2}$ hours before to 1 hour after H.W.) and groped our way through the early mists up the Seine. The new bridge spanning the river at Tancarville was certainly a marvellous sight. Ocean-going ships can pass beneath it; it provides a much-needed link between each bank at this point and is the only bridge until one gets to Rouen, some 50 miles upriver. The old familiar names crept past me—Quillebeuf, Caudebec, where the bore is at its worst, La Mailleraye, La Bouille.

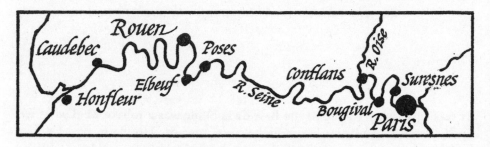

6. *The Maritime Seine, Paris to the Sea*

Rouen, a forest of gantries and ships' masts, came into view around 1700 and at 1745 we were fast in our same old berth just below the first bridge and thus, technically, still in the maritime section of the river.

It would be wrong to say that the efficiency of the French in Rouen had improved. It was most difficult to find the right police station at which to report for the passports to be stamped. But when, after three unsuccessful attempts based on wrong information from policemen, I managed to get them done, the courtesy of the officials took all the wind of protest out of my sails. With the Customs, matters had evidently changed. I have been no fewer than four times through France in a yacht, each time carrying a fair quantity of dutiable stores, and each time I have been most reasonably treated. The only formality was that the stores should be counted and subject to a recheck on emerging at the other end, to see how much was left and thus ensure that no 'traffic' had been taking place. Not so, how-ever, on this my fifth visit. After finally finding the right Customs office and persuading a rather reluctant Customs man to board our ship, he declared that either we must pay the full French duty or leave the lot behind. Faced with these two grim alternatives, we gave way to a show of some emotion, which gouged out of him the admission that, as we were passing the whole way through France, we might be allowed to employ a transit agent to have the stuff sent to Marseille and pick it up there.

It took a little while to locate a transit agent who would do such a small job and it looked at one point as though we were going to fail altogether. But at last a man was found and, after an all-day wait for him to come back, which he never did, and finally a frantic taxi drive to the railway station, he was located and, in exchange for our stores, gave us a piece of paper wherewith to claim them in Marseille. This operation cost NF. 72 (about £6 and we knew we would have to pay a lot more on reaching Marseille). I was, I admit, informed that I could make an impassioned plea to the Chief of the Customs, but was advised that this was not likely to better things. It seemed that the reason for this new and harsh Customs treatment was that about a year previously a 'British' yacht, or at least one of those many curious craft that somehow manage to fly a Red Ensign but none of whose crew speak any English, had passed through Rouen with a large amount of dutiable goods aboard and had been allowed to proceed to the Mediterranean in the usual way. After reaching Port St Louis and the open sea, however, she had a while later put back up the Rhône and sold her stores in Avignon. This had naturally been traced back to her and the French Customs had been obliged to rule that henceforth all yachts must tranship their stores by a transit agent. Thus the many must suffer for the follies of the few. 'Yachts' that behave like this should be severely punished and their names should be made public.

We were also required to get hold of a 'Permis de Circulation' for the canals at the Rouen Bureau de Navigation on the Ile Croix. Another taxi drive had to happen, only to find that the office was closed for lunch. At our second attempt, we were told that this office did not issue canal permits, which would have to be obtained in Paris. It did, however, give me a permit to proceed up the Seine to the first lock at Poses; we were never asked for this permit. Fortunately, I had, before leaving my home port, managed to get the A.A. to issue me with a 'Carnet de Passages en Douane' such as one gets when one takes one's car abroad, and this enabled the yacht to pass into French inland waters without further formality. I had often scoffed at the idea of such a document for a yacht, but was now glad to have it, as without it I would have had to persuade the local branch of Barclays Bank to issue me an indemnity before such a carnet could have been given. On the whole, things in France seemed to have tightened up considerably since I last cruised there. As for information, the same lack of it persisted.

As a result of all these delays and the nervous prostration they entailed, we missed the tide upriver and did not finally leave—against the current—until late that afternoon. We made a good deal of our passage upstream at dead low water and at one point I actually touched bottom, a thing I have never before done in the Seine. We managed to get as far as Elbeuf—a dreary little town where I gathered that they made blankets (wet or dry?), where we made fast for the night.

Our spirits had well recovered by next morning, when we made a seven-o'clock start and an hour and a half later (tide adverse again) we found ourselves waiting to enter the first lock at Poses. For some miles before getting to the lock we had been fighting our way through what seemed to be icebergs, but which were, in fact, nothing worse than great foamy floes of detergent from some local plant.

Progress throughout the day was excellent, the weather was glorious and the lock-keepers all helpful. In fact, when we arrived—well after the official closing time of 1900—at the last lock of the day at Carrières and wanted very much to lock through, the chief lock-keeper came along personally and saw to it that the gates were opened for us. I was much impressed. We sailed through in great style and made fast just the other side at the quay of the excellent clubhouse of the Cercle de la Voile de Paris at Meulan. The club boatman did everything possible to be nice to us and showed us around the first-class buildings. Next morning some of the club officers appeared and invited us to 'un Scotch' ashore, a hospitable act which we were able to repay aboard before sailing. I took the opportunity of replacing their courtesy flag—a Union Jack—by a Red Ensign out of ship's stores. I can confidently recommend this excellent and friendly club as a place to spend the night—or even longer—to any yachtsman passing up or down the Seine.

We slipped from Meulan soon after midday and at about 1500 made fast at Conflans-St Honorins, where the Oise joins the Seine, to a B.P. fuel barge to top up with diesel. It is, of course, uselessly expensive to ask for marine diesel oil anywhere in France now and has been so ever since the concession to pleasure craft to obtain duty-free fuel was withdrawn. But the French have got around this in their usual splendid Gallic way by offering what is locally known as 'fuel domestique', which is virtually the same as top-quality diesel fuel, except that it contains an infinitesimal extra amount of sulphur and is coloured pink. I paid Old Francs 21.40 per litre for it at Conflans and this is about what you expect to pay for it everywhere. Real diesel oil at inland prices would have been about four times as expensive. Engineers tell me that it is as well—though not vitally necessary —to mix a gallon of the well-known Vigzol compound called 'vitasul' into every 150 gallons of 'fuel domestique' shipped. This had the effect, in my case, of assuring absolute normality and at the same time of reducing smell and smoke to almost nil proportions.

There was a long delay at Bougival locks. I was going to press on regardless in search of somewhere suitable to spend the night. From time to time one saw a riverside notice warning that, instead of the usual 'keep to the right' rule, one would have to keep to the left, but there was never a notice to say that you should now keep to the right again. To some extent we were saved by observing the blue flags worn by the descending traffic on the side on which they wished you to pass (an international custom on European waterways), but I had not always the greatest confidence in such signals.

It had been a mistake not to stop the night at Bougival, for soon the river became wholly commercialized and we eventually—in sheer despair —made fast to a barge at an industrial suburb of Paris called Argenteuil.

This was, however, not without its advantages, for the barge skipper gave us an explanation of the curious river signs we had been noting all day with some perplexity. These took the forms of + and × on the river banks. He told us that + denoted 'navigation reversed', that is, a deviation from the normal right-hand to a left-hand course. The sign ×, on the other hand, indicated 'resume right-hand navigation'. He added that these signs were at that time in existence between Montereau, on the Upper Seine, down to Rouen as an experiment. He thought that they would probably prove a success and would be adopted permanently. I was glad to hear this, for I have long thought that something of the kind seemed necessary if accidents were to be avoided at the awkward parts of the river.

An early start next day, which was very warm and close, a lengthy passage through the lock at Suresnes, where the lock-keeper obligingly let me telephone to the Touring Club de France in Paris to give our E.T.A. and measurements to secure a berth, breakfast alongside a club barge at St Cloud, the ever-inspiring sight of the Eiffel Tower at Point du Jour and at 1100 we were fast at a T.C.F. berth near the Place de la Concorde, Paris. The 181 sea-miles and eight locks from Honfleur to Paris had taken four and a half sunny days. Since I made this trip, the locks at Les Mureaux and Port Villez on the lower Seine have been suppressed. This is a boon to all travellers on the river. I would estimate that the trip from Le Havre to Paris by river has thus been shortened from the 4½ days we always used to allow for it by at least half a day.

'If we go by the Burgundy route, can we possibly get through the tunnel?'—'Why, certainly. At least, I expect so. Well, of course, you may not. Frankly, I have no idea.' This about summed up the situation so far as knowledge of the Souterrain de Pouilly (as the tunnel in the summit level of the Canal de Bourgogne is called) was concerned in Paris.

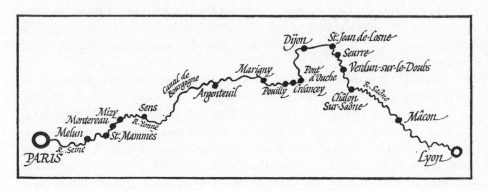

7. The Burgundy Route from Paris to Lyon

The headroom dimensions of the canal, according to a letter I had received from the Dijon branch of the Ponts et Chaussées (Public Works Department) were 3.50 m. (about 11 ft 7½ in.) beneath the bridges and 3.40 m. (about 11 ft 2½ in.) in the tunnel. The maximum permissible dimensions for craft navigating this waterway, according to other French official sources, were:

Length	38.50 m. (126 ft 2 in.)
Beam	5.00 m. (16 ft 5 in.)
Draught	1.80 m. (5 ft 11 in.)
Freeboard at centre	3.20 m. (10 ft 6 in.)
Freeboard at sides	2.20 m. (7 ft 3 in.)

We came well within all of these except for the freeboard, where we seemed to be an inch or two too tall at the centre, but we put our trust in the Dijon figures, which gave a much more optimistic picture.

Nobody at the Touring Club de France seemed very certain of the situation, nor, when I went to fetch my 'Permis de Circulation' for the canals, were the people at the Ministry of Public Works. We reflected that it would indeed be something of an anticlimax if we got as far as the Pouilly Tunnel—142 locks away—and had to come back and try another route. We asked some of the other yachtmen in Paris what they thought, but either they were going no farther (in which case they didn't know or care), or they were going another route and were too concerned with the problems of their own canals to start worrying about other people's.

There were no port dues to pay in Paris, as we did not stay longer than the two days allowed free of charge. We had to pay, of course, for the rent of the telephone that was placed aboard (well worth it) and give reasonable tips for fresh water and other attentions, but the service was very good (except perhaps for the telephone exchange!) and we did not feel we had been robbed. The staff of the Touring Club de France were as courteous as on our last visit two or three years ago. I am sorry to say that their knowledge of their own waterways was as limited as ever. But the facilities had improved and the berthing arrangements were good. We were lucky to run into an Englishman, Mr Eric Field, a former naval C.P.O., running a sort of yacht-broking business in Paris, who helped us a lot with stores.

Midday on May 14 saw us passing the soaring twin towers of Notre-Dame upriver. The locks on the Upper Seine were at their worst, crowded and subject to endless delays, some of them quite inexplicable. We often had to wait an hour before entering and then it took another hour or so to lock through. The keepers seemed as exasperated as anyone by the slowness of the whole thing: I was delighted to hear from one of them that works were being prepared to suppress half the locks on the Upper Seine. As this would involve a subsequent rise in the general level of the river of over 6 ft, the job needed to be carefully prepared.

The rule in France is that during the summer months the locks operate until 1930. If, however, the opening of a lock would involve working beyond this limit, the lock simply does not start to open. Thus, although we arrived at Citanguettes Lock—about 28 miles from Paris—at 1830, traffic at the time was coming from the opposite direction and we knew that there was no hope of us getting through that night. So we made fast at a private quay downstream. The owners were apparently delighted to see us, even going so far as to hoist a courtesy flag for us, and at once invited us up to their house, where we spent a wonderful evening together.

A start was made next morning—as indeed every other day from now onwards—at 0630, the hour when navigation officially commences. Progress was again painfully slow, although it got a bit quicker after passing the entrance to the Canal du Loing at St Mammès. This doubtless drained off some of the traffic. The folding map of the Upper Seine from Paris to Montereau which we had bought was shown often to be misleading. Near Samois, for instance, it showed a row of red buoys as marking dangers off-lying the left bank, whereas in fact they lay off the right. We were only saved from following its disastrous advice by observing what course others were taking. Water-level generally was low and in the pound between Melun and La Cave our 5 ft deep keel was often in the mud.

At Montereau we left the Seine and turned right into the River Yonne, which seemed at least as broad as the Seine and with about as much water in it, although the depths varied considerably from pound to pound, some of them having so little that we often seemed to scrape along the muddy bottom, others having (according to the echo-sounder) a good 20 ft of water in them. The night was spent at Mizy, strategically placed to enter the lock next morning.

Our second and last day in the Yonne saw good progress and mercifully little traffic. It was therefore possible to enter the locks rapidly, although locking through was often a long job, due to the very great length of the lock and the slowness of the water entry. Their side walls, too, were shelving, so that the ship's sides often bumped. When the water had finally risen to its full extent, the yacht was always marooned well away from the sides, so that casting off presented difficulties. Why locks were built in this absurd way is beyond me.

We could not resist stopping for an hour or two at Sens, the only town of any significance on the Yonne, where we went to see the superb small cathedral with the relics of Thomas à Becket. That evening, with thunder-clouds gathering in the still air, we arrived at Laroche-Migennes and left the Yonne for the Canal de Bourgogne. The number of the lock—115— showed us what tribulations lay between us and the summit.

We had only passed six locks next morning when we came upon a bridge marked 'Headroom only 3.40 metres', thus showing how absurdly in-accurate the official information had been. We stopped and removed the headlight from the coach-house roof. Three locks previously we had been forced for the same reason to remove the dinghy davits while in a lock (this was considered the easiest way). From then onwards we went ahead with greater confidence, although we several times were within an ace of removing the loud-hailer from our roof, which would have given us another 3 or 4 in. clearance.

We soon noticed that the bollards for making fast in the locks were all built on the opposite side to the lock-keepers' houses, so we altered our lines to come starboard side to each time. There was usually one older person— often a woman—to operate each lock. This meant that, unless one wanted to wait a month of Sundays two of our ship's company of four had to jump ashore and give a hand. The locks were all easy, there was seldom a very great rise and fall, and although we started cautiously, taking about 7 to 8 minutes to negotiate each lock, we were soon down to an average of 5 minutes per lock and on two unforgettable occasions we actually reduced the time to 4, which, of course, called for drinks all round. Traffic was mercifully light, only one barge being encountered all day: and he was bribed with cigarettes to let us pass him.

Next day we broke all records by passing through no fewer than fifty-six locks. Certainly I have never done such a thing in all my 'ditch-crawling' days and I doubt if anyone has surpassed this. This was made possible by the almost complete absence of traffic, the fine teamwork that we were now showing and to the absence of distractions *en route* which could have per-suaded us to stop. Many of the locks were very close together, so that one of us could run ahead and get things started before the boat herself arrived.

I need hardly say that on arrival we dined ashore that night. The place was called Marigny.

I must confess our nerves were a little frayed next morning as we approached the Pouilly Tunnel. Some of the bargees and lock-keepers had said we hadn't a hope of getting through and others had encouraged us to go on and have a stab at it. We passed through the mile-long Tranchée de Creuzot, a narrow pound with high rocks overhanging it, and at length Lock No. 1, the last of our arduous uphill climb, came into sight, and beyond it the summit level and the tunnel.

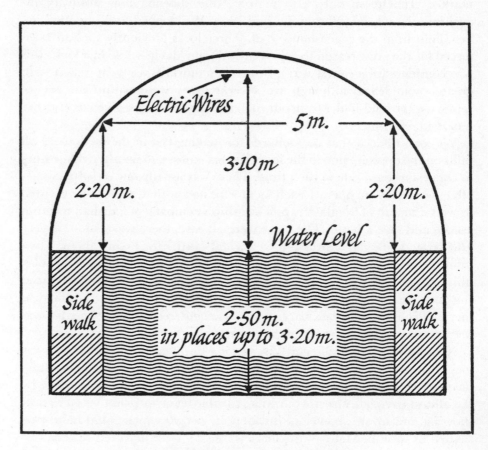

8. The Pouilly Tunnel in cross-section

We had hurried to be in time for the south-going convoy starting at 1345, which we imagined we would have to join, but the lock-keeper told us that, as there was no traffic that day, there was consequently no convoy either and that, in any case, yachts could pass unaccompanied. In fact, he told us a whole lot of things, which I place on record here for the benefit of others who may make the self-same journey:

1. All yachts may pass through in either direction under their own power. No need to take the electric tug.

2. The electric tug leaves her base at Pouilly daily at 0715 and 1345, according to demand and returns from Créancey (the other end of the tunnel) as required. Barges are compelled to use the tow.

3. The telephone numbers of the two terminals are: Pouilly-en-Auxois 84 and Créancey 3.

4. The tariff to pass the tunnel was as follows: 230-ton barges (laden), NF. 18.44; 230-ton barges (light), NF. 15.75; 120- to 230-ton barges (laden), NF. 13.83; 120- to 230-ton barges (light), NF. 11.81; barges up to 120 tons (laden), NF. 9.22; barges up to 120 tons (light), NF. 7.88. To this must be added small amounts for stamps. Presumably, all yachts passing this way would qualify as 'barges below 120 tons, light'.

5. The dimensions of the tunnel are given in the accompanying sketch.

6. The normal minimum depth of water is 2.50 m., but in places in the tunnel it is as much as 3.20 m. The water-level can be lowered considerably (from the Créancey end) to enable the freeboard to be increased.

7. Three wires to give power for the electric tug run overhead in the centre of the arch, about 3 in. beneath it. These continue for some distance outside the tunnel and vessels in doubt regarding freeboard available can test it by placing themselves beneath these wires.

8. The best way of making the passage is to shine the ship's searchlight on the wires and steer on them.

9. The length of the tunnel is 3,257 m. and it is unlit.

We paid our dues and the assistant keeper said we would be wise to take advantage of the scheme for lowering the water-level. We agreed, and he bicycled off to the other end of the tunnel to see to things, while we made fast at the end of the cutting leading to the tunnel and waited for about an hour while they lowered the water. At length, it seemed safe to pass and, with hearts beating, we entered the vault. It was a bit of a struggle getting through. One of us sat on deck holding the searchlight trained on the wires and freezing to death, while the rest of us, stifling with heat and excitement, remained in the wheelhouse at the wheel and watching the sides, which at times seemed perilously close. The passage took us exactly 47 minutes, proceeding at about 3 knots, and we were jolly glad to get through and see our lock-keeper, whom I tipped NF. 10 for his pains.

From then onwards the whole character of the journey changed. Instead of toiling laboriously uphill, we sank noiselessly down, never bothering to make fast our lines to the lock bollards. There was never work for more than two, so that the rest of us could take it easy or even get some much-needed walking along the towpath from lock to lock. The only snag was that, since it is canal practice to leave locks open to receive upcoming traffic rather than downgoing, we found the locks all closed against us as we arrived and often had to wait while the ladies in charge rushed frantically around preparing for us. To get over this, we hired a small boy with a bicycle who, for a moderate reward, obligingly went ahead along the towpath and cried for us in the wilderness.

The night was spent at Pont d'Ouche, a delightful Côte d'Or village where they refused to accept money for the bread (this made a great impression), and next day before starting we actually got hold of a boy with a motor-cycle who preceded us at a great speed and got us to Dijon well before dinner. We paid him NF. 10 and NF. 5 for his lunch. The canal in these parts was very winding and once we very nearly had a collision with a solitary barge, only avoided by both of us going hard astern for some time.

Dijon is a magnificent town. The fame of its mustard has unfortunately rather outrun that of its historic buildings, the impact of whose beauty came as something of a surprise to us. But the canal there is a dark and smelly affair and we were glad to leave early next morning, having, as usual, hired a boy with a bike to go before us. The canal leg between Dijon and its debouchment into the River Saône at St Jean de Losne is almost dead straight through relatively flat country. There was a bit more traffic than to date, but nothing serious and the one barge that threatened to delay us was conveniently bribed with twenty cigarettes to stop and let us pass him. We met up with two dumb-barges filled with gravel and hauled by diesel tractors on the towpath, an unexpectedly picturesque encounter, though not so reminiscent as the 'Berrichons' we had seen on the Canal Latéral à la Loire, and drawn by a mixed mule and horse team, a few years earlier. Our motorized herald worked so well that we arrived at the last lock—No. 76—leading into the River Saône, by lunch-time and were able to put our dinghy davits back into position.

There was general rejoicing at St Jean, where the man at the fuel pump actually recognized me. We watered and topped up with 'fuel domestique' at NF. 0.217 per litre. We all had hot baths aboard, a relaxed lunch and sailed feeling pretty good. We passed through two of the river locks before eventually making fast for Saturday night at Seurre, where we all went sound asleep in the cinema out of sheer exhaustion. A Monsieur Berger, a transport king with a house alongside our berth, was very good to us with information and advice.

Sunday's start was mercifully late and the voyage along the Saône's upper reaches was most agreeable. At the big new lock at Verdun-sur-le-Doubs, we met with another British motor yacht, *Mullion* (Messrs Metherell and Liddell-Simpson), with whom we were able to trade a bottle of good old Scotch for two bottles of Pouilly-Fumé, which brought back memories of the tunnel rather sharply.

Disdaining a halt to take a pilot at Châlon-sur-Saône, we pushed on to arrive that night at Tournus, one of the prettiest and most historic towns on the Saône. I was in two minds whether a pilot was necessary or not. Once before I had been aground in the Saône below Tournus, but the water-level then had been a good bit lower than it was now, so that the mean streak in me prevailed. Nevertheless, at Tournus I made inquiries in the riverside cafés and found that one was available if required, though at a figure I thought unreasonable and probably not in accord with the official tariff.

My 'Leadsman' did us yeoman service at the places where I knew there was little water and the next day's leg passed without disaster. I was particularly careful in the reach just above the fine white buildings of the Yacht Club du Rhône, where I had spent a humiliating 3 hours aground in 1957, and at the approaches to Bernalin Locks, where the river plan gives the wrong instructions. I was glad to note that the locks at Couzon had been entirely rebuilt, so that their passage no longer involves the very long waits that used to happen. The wait at Ile Barbe Locks, however, was worse than ever. I see from my log that we took 75 minutes to pass this one. Our ill temper when at last they let us in was somewhat relieved by the news that this lock was to be reconstructed very soon.

It is certainly a good thing that these ancient Saône locks should be rebuilt or suppressed, as the delays used to be intolerable and the volume of traffic the river carries certainly justifies some expenditure. In Lyon, we lay at our usual berth by the Pont de Tilsitt. I had telephoned our old friend Pariset, pilote du Rhône, asking for his services next day. His assistant, Henri Morvent, duly appeared and we fixed a date for him to board us at 0545. Lyon has probably the best food in the world, so that evening a good blow-out was had by all.

Henri Morvent, our pilot, duly came aboard at 0545; and at 0600 we slipped from the Quai de Tilsitt in Lyon and slid gently down the Saône to the lock at La Mulatière, where the Saône and Rhône converge.

There was some delay in the lock while papers were being filled, so we took the opportunity of watering and went along to check the water-level in the Rhône at the gauge by the lockside. This showed a depth of 3.7 m., falling. As we knew from our previous trips down the Rhône that we were safe—with our draught of 1.5 m.—to navigate it with a least depth of only 3.1 m., we felt doubly assured. But the fact that everyone admitted the level was falling confirmed us in our determination to get under way as soon as possible. The awkward part in the Rhône navigation is the stretch from Lyon down to the point above Valence where the River Isère flows into the Rhône with its additional water from the Alps and Val d'Isère. After that, all is usually plain sailing, but I have often seen strings of vessels waiting at this point for more water to proceed upstream.

With the pilot at the wheel and the ship's company relaxing in the early sunshine, it was as pleasant a Rhône trip as any I have experienced. I first sailed down this river in 1955 and was towed back up it in 1956. There had been changes each time and I was deeply interested to see how things were in 1960. Certainly, at that particular point, things seemed the same as ever —the same brown swirling waters, the same jagged rocks on either bank and the same unceasing vigilance at the wheel to keep her on course. At one bend, the pilot—I thought rather proudly—pointed out the wreck of a small motor yacht ashore. Her owner, he explained, had decided against

9. Bingen showing confluence of the River Nahe with the Rhine and a passenger steamer approaching the Maüseturm Signal station.

10. At Duisburg in the heart of the Ruhr. *Dame des Iles* at her most industrial berth.

11. Rushing down the Rhône. The rock is the famous Table du Roi.

12. At Poses Lock on the Lower Seine. The 'icebergs' are floes of detergent waste from a nearby plant.

13. 80 ft down in Bollène Lock.

14. Entering the new lock at Montelimar.

15. About to ascend the famous Seven Locks in the Midi Canal.

16. The picturesque medieval approach to La Rochelle harbour. In olden days the port used to be closed by stretching a chain between the two towers.

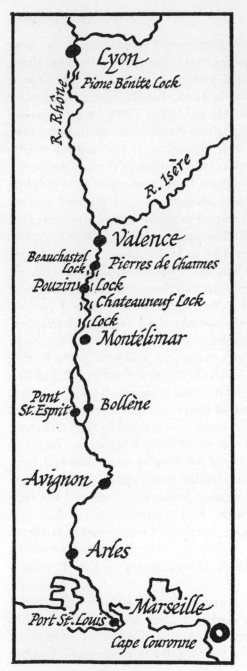

taking a pilot. Duly impressed, I could not resist a photograph of this solemn warning.

At Valence, the current with its estimated 16 km.p.h. still ran as fast as ever, building up against the bridge arches in great choco-late-coloured humps.

When we arrived at the notorious Pierres de Charmes, where in 1956 we had taken almost the whole of one afternoon to negotiate the rapids in tow upstream, I was comforted to see that work had recently started on the building of a new combined lock and hydro-electric project. There was the usual 8-knot current running over the shallow, rocky river bed. It will be a great blessing to Rhône navi-gation when this spot is eventually by-passed—almost as much of a blessing as was the by-passing of the infamous passage of Pont Saint-Esprit when the first big locks at Bollène (Donzère-Mon-dragon project) were built. My pilot told me that no fewer than three of the big petrol barges of the Citerna company had recently gone aground at Pierres de Char-mes.

At about 1330, just as I had finished an excellent lunch, we entered the approach canal to the

9. Lyon to Port St Louis

new locks at Pouzin. These had only been opened to navigation five days previously and we thus had the honour of being the first yacht to use them. Six kilometres later (to be precise, at Kilometre 141 measured from Lyon) we made fast at the entrance to Pouzin Lock. Pouzin exercises the same attitude towards pleasure craft as do the other big Rhône locks: you are only privileged to pass if in company with a commercial craft. Otherwise, the locks will not operate. This rule, however, is not always strictly applied, especially if your pilot happens to be a chum of the lock-keepers.

In fact, we had to wait about half an hour, made fast to a dolphin, before a couple of barges arrived downstream, entered the lock and we were called in after them. Our pilot was on excellent terms with one of the barge skippers, who came along and offered me a tow down the 20-odd km. of canal between Pouzin and the next lock at Montélimar. The pilot urged me to accept, since, he said, if we did not keep up with the barges, we would never get to the next lock in time to pass through it in company with them. I therefore accepted, albeit rather half-heartedly, for I had no experience of this sort of thing and was not sure what was likely to happen.

We accordingly unshipped our longest and stoutest line, which the barge made fast to her stern and we to our samson post and winch. On leaving the lock, all seemed well and the line took the strain gallantly. But in a flash the barge had increased speed—I imagine to about 26 km.p.h. (about 13 knots)—and our bow was well out of the water. As there was no run of river current to help us on our way, there was a considerable difference between my 8 knots and his 13. I was wondering whether we ought to abandon this rather curious tow, when my doubts were removed by a smell of smoke forward. Our line, under the great strain, had somehow worked loose and the wood of the samson post was smoking as the rope chafed around it. The anchor winch, I afterwards noticed, had also worked slightly loose on its base. Our horrified shouts quickly attracted the attention of the barge crew, her skipper eased her down, she cast off the tow and we dropped thankfully astern. It was only then that I realized how foolish we had been.

The 22 km. of canalized Rhône between Pouzin and Montélimar (at Kilometre 163) were put astern in exactly 1 hour and 40 minutes, thus giving a speed of about 13 km.p.h., against nearly twice this rate of advance in the river proper. There was only a very small run of current—I would not estimate it at more than 2 knots (say 4 km.p.h.) and the channel was clearly buoyed throughout. The buoys had luminous topmarks for night navigation.

There was only a 15-minute wait at Montélimar Lock—also new to me since my last Rhône passage—so that our haste to take a tow proved super-fluous. We continued through the calm of the canal for another 27 km. from Montélimar to Bollène (Donzère project) at Kilometre 190, where we again had only a quarter of an hour to wait before passing into and through this, the deepest of the three great Rhône locks now in use. Our rate of advance in the canal between Montélimar and Donzère had been exactly the same as in the previous section. A few minutes after leaving Bollène, we arrived at the celebrated Kilometre 200 mark and found our-selves once more in the Rhône proper. As they swirled around us after our tranquil canal passage, the laughing waters seemed to welcome us back, chiding us for having left them and challenging us once again to take up the southward struggle.*

There were no more canals or locks after Kilometre 200 and the rest of the passage down towards Avignon, accomplished in the gathering dusk, was just the same as in the old days when the torrent held full sway. The only exception was that a few kilometres above Avignon the river had been buoyed for the first time in history. When I first sighted one of these buoys heeling over in the current with only its top and a bit of its side showing, I thought it must be a body or a piece of floating wreckage impaled on a rock, so small was it. This excellent innovation leads the whole way from above Avignon down to Port St Louis du Rhône, where one leaves the river for the sea.

* It is only proper to add that, at the time of this book's going to press (1967), two more giant locks have been opened to traffic on the Rhône. The latest position is therefore that, in addition to those of Bollène (sometimes known as Donzère-Mondragon) and Pouzin (also known as Baix-Logis-Neuf), the locks at Chateauneuf, near Le Teil, between Pouzin and Bollène, and those at Beauchastel (upstream from Pouzin) are now function-ing. Furthermore, the Pierre Bénite locks, close downriver from Lyon, is expected to open in 1967, which presumably would mean suppressing the La Mulatière Locks at the junction of the Saône and Rhône Rivers.

This is all highly gratifying and brings the day nearer when not only will traffic flow unimpeded between Lyon and the sea but the anxieties of pilotage and towage will dis-appear for ever on this great river. Meanwhile, one of the obvious advantages is that up-stream navigation becomes easier and quicker. Conversely, of course, a downstream passage takes longer because of the extra locks—but 'it's an ill wind . . .'

It was almost dark when, making a half-turn against the stream, we came alongside the quay at Avignon for the night. Henri Morvent left us and took the train back to Lyon, refreshed by a meal and a bottle of something. We paid him his fee of NF. 180, now standard for the Lyon–Arles leg, and he went on his way rejoicing, having arranged for a relief man to come aboard next day and take us down the remaining 20 miles to Arles. The fee we had already paid took care also of this extra leg.

There is always plenty to see in Avignon, even on one's fourth visit by boat to the city, and the forenoon was very easily filled in with sightseeing. At 1500 the pilot duly boarded us and we swung out past the famous incomplete Pont d'Avignon and were on our way to Arles. It was another delightful afternoon run, easy boating with the river buoyed all the way, and I began to wonder whether it would soon be considered unnecessary to take a pilot between Avignon and Arles. Perhaps the few rapid stretches near Avignon still make it a wise precaution.

At Arles, we swung around and berthed bows to the current on the western bank of the river alongside a barge. This is the berth where a yacht is least disturbed, since, although it is perhaps inconveniently placed for shopping and sightseeing, there is almost no movement of the traffic. On the other side, the barges move frequently and a yacht can get the worst of the bargain. At Arles, the pilot left us.

Looking back on this, my first trip through the Burgundy route, I came easily to the conclusion that, were I taking any of the three central routes through France to reach the Mediterranean, I would certainly plump for the Burgundy if my vessel were capable of getting through the Pouilly Tunnel. Granted, there are far more locks than on the other routes, but there is very much less traffic. In fact, the traffic on the canal itself was almost nil. Whether this was normal or whether it was due to the fact that a *chômage* (period of canal closure for cleaning) was imminent, I cannot say, but the odds are that it is always like that.

Arles to Marseille can easily be made in a day if you start early. We slipped at 0700 and had an easy and pleasant trip down the Rhône, our masts raised again for the first time since we left Paris. The red-and-white horizontally marked buoys were of the greatest help, especially in the few delicate places near Arles, and we made Port St Louis about 3 hours later. The red flag barring entry to the lock was conveniently not flying and we went straight in. Although the bridge over it was down, the lock itself was not closed and the river was surging through unchecked, so that, when we were invited to go through into the outer basin for clearance, we found ourselves caught in the current and took a while to get alongside again.

Clearance at Port St Louis is always fun. The Customs and Immigration have a keen sense of humour. But it was not so funny to have to walk a mile or so to get the passports stamped on technically leaving France. Maybe, in any case, this was not necessary, but it is always good to be on the safe side.

On leaving Port St Louis, there followed about 1½ miles of seaway known as the Canal de Port St Louis and we were then in the open sea. Scorning the inland route to Marseille across the Golfe de Fos and through the Rove Tunnel, we took the open sea route around Cape Couronne, giving our E.T.A. as 1530. *September Tide* clove the Mediterranean gratefully like a bird released from bondage.

It had certainly been a more entertaining way down through France than either the 'Bourbonnais' or the Marne routes.

I have described our passage south through the 'Bourbonnais' in Chapter 1. The Marne route we had done in May/June 1957 in *September Tide*. Physically, it had been a good deal less exhausting than either of the other two ways south; there had been only 161 locks to cope with, against 178 by the 'Bourbonnais' and 254 by the 'Bourgogne', despite a slightly longer mileage.

On that particular occasion I remembered how we had reached Paris after negotiating the lower reaches of the Seine in early May and, after the usual local junketings and the collection of a crew, had set forth upstream in good heart.

We lowered our masts again—we had raised them in Paris to create a good impression—and set off upstream in the afternoon of May 14. In under an hour we had reached the junction of the Marne with the Seine and turned left into the Marne. This junction is not always easy to find and I can well imagine anyone overshooting the mark if they had not kept a sharp look-out for it.

Five minutes later we were in our first lock on the new route south. From then onwards we paid very special attention to the folding map of the Marne that we had bought. It was not always entirely clear, with the result that we at one stage overshot the entrance to a short cut by-passing a great deal of the very sinuous Marne—a short cut known as the St Maur tunnel. The kilometre posts soon put us right, however, and we realized our mistake and put about, locking into the approach to the tunnel with a barge. The lock-keeper here was far from pleasant—an unusual spectacle. He demanded to see our 'Autorisation de Circulation', a piece of bureaucracy which I never bother to obtain, saying that the mere possession of a Customs *laissez-passer* was insufficient. Finally, seeing that we were as obstinate as he, and were holding up the traffic at his lock, he agreed to let us pass and we never heard any more about this useless piece of paper the length and breadth of France. That night we stopped at a hamlet called Neuilly-sur-Marne and the lockside café-keeper presented us with a small tortoiseshell kitten called Mousse. He was just fourteen days old.

Next day we made excellent progress. The river was perfectly beautiful, the lock-keepers helpful and polite, and there was very little traffic. The result was that we covered almost 100 km.—and passed ten easy locks—in the $10\frac{1}{2}$ hours we were under way. It was such a long day that we decided next day to give ourselves an easier time—only putting in 7 hours' steaming and stopping at Chateau Thierry *en route* for some shopping. We were, nevertheless, to arrive that evening at Epernay, the first lock taking us out of the Marne and into the first of the canals we were to use, known as the Canal Latéral à la Marne. Fresh water and fuel (price Frs 19 a litre) were both available here, but we thought it wiser to wait until later before replenishing.

We were now in the region of low, fixed bridges and, with the aid of some well-disposed bargees, we made some tests of our wheelhouse top, according to which we would just scrape through the rest of the canal.

Our first day in the canal proved frustrating. By 1000, some $2\frac{1}{2}$ hours after starting, we joined the Aisne–Marne Canal and traffic was heavy. There were endless waits and in the late afternoon we had the misfortune to find ourselves astern of a very slow and very large barge which proceeded ahead of us for hours. The pounds were just too short for us to overtake him and the whole journey became a nightmare of delays and impatience. Nevertheless, we managed to make Vitry-le-François, where we knew the Aisne–Marne Canal would disentangle itself from us, by the end of the day. Here we fuelled at Frs 22.20 per litre and embarked some fresh water. I had a chill and a high temperature, so it was decided to call a doctor, get some suitable tablets and to give the morrow a miss.

By 1000 on May 19 the wretched captain was pronounced by his impatient crew well enough to continue and we turned thankfully out of the Canal Latéral à la Marne into the long Canal de la Marne à la Saône, which was to be our home for some days. This involved, first of all, passing beneath a very low railway bridge, where we found to our horror that parts of our superstructure were actually touching. On getting through, the lock-keeper told us that it allowed for a 3.50 m. freeboard (11.4 ft), but I am sure this was not so. Conditions thereafter improved greatly, although the numbering of the locks was obviously designed to mystify us, and we were able to put 44 km. and eighteen locks behind us that day. In the area of St Dizier, close to where we eventually made fast for the night, the canal was a glorious russet brown from a near-by tannery.

From a purely lock point of view, the day that followed was our greatest triumph to date, for we accounted for no fewer than twenty-seven of them, giving us another 62 km. forward. The day's high spot was the low bridge at Joinville. We came on it as we swung round a bend and immediately reduced speed—mercifully as it proved, for it had several notices written up on it in chalk by altruistic bargees, calling attention to its low head-room. We got half-way beneath it, only to find that our searchlight and dinghy davits were all scratching on it. We stopped everything and, in some alarm, I thought of going along to the lock-keeper and asking him to let some water out of the pound and so bring us down a few inches. Short of this, I could think of no means of getting us out of our fix, other perhaps than by asking twenty or thirty of the heftier citizens of Joinville to board us and weigh us down, for I knew that our davits could not be got out of their sockets without a major mechanical operation.

However, good fortune smiled on us, for, by dint of pulling down our dinghy davits—which luckily had some 'give' in them—we were able just to squeeze our way beneath the bridge and go on our way. A crowd of locals had, of course, gathered to gaze at our efforts. They told us, with what truth I do not know, that the Germans had built the bridge and that the Americans had repaired it—thus disclaiming all French responsibility. At the following lock, the keeper told us that, at that day's water-level in the pound of 2.25 m., there was a clearance below the bridge of 3.36 m.

(about 11 ft), which was exactly our own freeboard. He assured us that there were no more bridges with such a low clearance and we went on our way rejoicing. That night was spent at a little place called Riaucourt, whose only claim to note seemed to be that everyone was in bed by eight o'clock.

Next day provided us with a great landmark, in that we reached the summit level of the Canal de la Marne à la Saône (340 m. or about 1,115 ft). We started early and found a most noteworthy absence of traffic, there being, in fact, none at all for the first sixteen locks. We became so used to quick lock passages that we found we were negotiating them at an average speed of 7 minutes per lock, timed from the moment the bows entered the lock to the moment they emerged from it. Around lunch-time we ran into a procession of five or six barges coming against us. From the keepers, we learned that this was the convoy that had passed through the tunnel in the summit level the previous night and this caused us to make inquiry about the laws governing this traffic.

We learned that southbound traffic such as we were, could be in the tunnel between 0000 and 0300 and between 1200 and 1500, whereas northbound traffic, such as the barges we had just encountered, had permission to be in the tunnel between 0800 and 1100 and between 2000 and 2300. There was no notice up indicating these rules and no one in Paris or elsewhere had told us anything about it, so that it was by sheer luck that we discovered it. Someone ought to take the officials of the Touring Club de France in Paris to task for the haphazard way in which yachts are allowed to sail from Paris down the canals without proper information. The only two barges we met that day going our way most politely allowed us to pass and we made excellent progress, passing through as many as twenty-nine locks before we found ourselves in the summit level at Batailles (near Langres).

It was then 1845. We knew from the lock-keeper that barges coming the other way had the right to enter the tunnel at 2000, so that this gave us only an hour and a quarter to pass through nearly 5 km. of tunnel and some 2 km. of canal leading to it. Darkness was not far off and I was for having a shot at it, but the prospect of meeting up with a northgoing barge whilst in it and consequently having to go astern perhaps for nearly 5 km. in the darkness of the narrows was too much for my crew and we cautiously decided to turn in until midnight, when we would have the right to an unhindered passage.

Midnight arrived and we were swathed in a thick mist. We could see the stars, but all around us swirled the mists of the fields of France. We groped our way forward and at last to our great joy found our searchlight illuminating the entrance to the tunnel. Once inside—and it was very narrow and low—we found the going much easier, though it was often quite a job to keep our sides from scraping on the walls. We emerged at Heuilley-Cotton an hour and twenty minutes later, with the tiresome conviction that we probably could just have done it if we had gone on our way the previous evening.

Next morning we breakfasted late, did some shopping and went on our way in the comfortable knowledge that the locks were now all downhill. It was nice to have them numbered from No. 1 onwards descending towards the River Saône, in the certainty that when we had passed No. 43 we would be done with canals. Despite our late start, we actually put twenty-eight locks behind us that day before stopping the night at Saint Seine.

Soon after lunch we arrived at Maxilly, Lock No. 43, and the last of the canal locks, and gave a cheer as we found ourselves at long last in the beautiful River Saône. The larger river locks of Heuilly, Poncey and Auxonne were easily negotiated and by that evening we found ourselves fast for the night at the friendly little hamlet of St Jean de Losne, where we would have emerged if we had taken the Canal de Bourgogne. The Saône in these upper reaches has plenty of water, almost no current and there are virtually no dangers, so that there was no thought of taking a pilot. At St Jean de Losne we watered from a convenient hose-pipe and shipped 250 litres of fuel at Frs 19 per litre.

A delightful day was spent running down the Saône to Chalon-sur-Saône, still pilotless, and in bright sunshine. There were four locks to pass, all fully manned, but each took some time, as we unluckily met some up-coming traffic.

At Chalon I decided, in view of the relatively low level of the river, to take a pilot. So I went ashore and investigated matters in the various waterside cafés. Three gentlemen offered their services, each with an appearance of qualification. I found that their fees were very similar, varying between Frs 10,000 and Frs 12,000 for the passage from Chalon to

Lyon. Eventually we clinched with a fellow called Pierre Thurillet, who was well spoken of, and he embarked next morning at daybreak.

I was glad I had taken him, for he proved a trustworthy man and I was not keen to repeat my experiences of the previous year, when, in a period of low water, I had twice found myself aground in this river, the lower reaches of which are fraught with uncertainties and for which the folding river plan that we carried is no reliable guide.

Passage downstream was extremely fast, and in sharp contradistinction to the long delays at the locks, at some of which we spent over an hour and a half. There were five locks and at Ile Barbe, the last lock before arriving at Lyon, poor old Thurillet, who had a train to catch back to Chalon, asked permission to abandon ship. I gladly gave this, as the remainder of the passage into Lyon was easily done, and he then made the surprising announcement that we did not owe him the Frs 11,000 for which we had contracted but only Frs 9,000, producing at the same time his official tariff list to explain why. It was clear from this that pilots on the Saône are entitled to Frs 9,000 for the trip between Chalon and Lyon, but receive an extra Frs 2,000 for taking you through the city of Lyon. I made a mental note for the future that if ever we went down the Saône again, I would drop my pilot before entering Lyon, for this to a yacht is perfectly easy and is certainly not worth Frs 2,000 of pilotage.

3

'Entre Deux Mers'

The Midi Short Cut between Two Seas

Yachtsmen rarely use the canals between Sète and Bordeaux. Nothing much is known about this route, whereas the standard canal passages to the Mediterranean via Paris and the Rhône are better known and easier to find out about. Ask a French official about the Midi Canals and he will shrug his shoulders. As for official maps and guides, they are almost impossible to obtain. It is for these reasons, coupled with the well-founded suspicion that the Canal du Midi—at any rate—is not an easy passage, that has made yachtsmen shy off the south-western canals as a whole.

After spending the summer in the Mediterranean, I was anxious to bring *September Tide* home to Jersey by some route other than the Rhône, which in any case would have cost me close on £100 for a tow upstream. I was too late to contemplate the long haul via Gibraltar with much equanimity, so I set myself the job of finding out about the Sète–Bordeaux route.

I was fortunate in having a pal in Cannes who skippered a French motor cruiser that used this route almost every season. He came around to have a look at my boat and said he thought we hadn't a hope of getting through. He added, however, that if we got through the lock and low bridge at Agde, soon after entering the canal, we were certain of getting through the rest of it. He added that, if we failed at Agde, we could always put about and use the branch canal at La Nouvelle, farther southward, and enter the main system by this means. If, however, we did this, we still would have to face the hazards of several more low bridges, notably at Toulouse.

Undaunted, I wrote a letter to the Ponts et Chaussées (the French canal

authority) at Sète, thinking that they at least must have the answer, and giving the dimensions of my craft. From them I had a helpful reply, which stated, *inter alia*, that the following were the maximum dimensions of a vessel to which a permit to navigate the Sète–Bordeaux canals would be given:

Length, 30 m. (98.4 ft); beam, 5.50 m. (18.04 ft); freeboard amidships, 3 m. (9.8 ft); freeboard at sides, 2 m. (6.6 ft); draught on Canal du Midi, 1.60 m. (5.27 ft); draught on Canal Latéral à la Garonne, 1.80 m. (5.92 ft).

The Canal du Midi links Sète with Toulouse, and the Canal Latéral à la Garonne links Toulouse with the River Garonne, whence Bordeaux is reached. Different permitted measurements are quoted for freeboard amidships and at sides, owing to the curvature of many of the canal bridges.

At the same time, I was informed that, before starting the voyage, I must obtain a 'Permis de Circulation', or permit to navigate the canals, from the Ponts et Chaussées office at Toulouse.

Armed with this information, my French skipper chum and I again checked our measurements, which, to his great surprise, proved that we came within these limits. Naturally, as well as dismasting ourselves, we would have to remove our dinghy and anchor davits and take the searchlight and loud-hailer off the wheelhouse roof, but this seemed little hardship. I thereupon wrote to the Ponts et

10. '*Entre Deux Mers*'

Chaussées office at Toulouse, again giving our measurements and at the same time asking, if they considered us to meet their requirements, to send us the necessary permit. This they shortly did, assuring us at the same time that we need have nothing to fear.

And so it was a great day when finally we sailed from Cannes that October. After two stops at St Tropez and Toulon due to bad weather (it was worse down there than later in the Bay), we made Marseille three days later. On passage we bade farewell to Grasse Radio, our prop and stay the whole of the summer, and changed our watch over to Marseille Radio. Though Marseille is still, for its size, a poor yacht harbour (even the fresh-water tap connections fail to fit the standard French fittings), it had at least improved in one respect. You could now obtain diesel fuel at the distribution point in the Vieux Port up to 300 litres (66 gallons) without the maddening formality of a visit to the main Customs office downtown with your ship's papers. This we did. We also tried to have a few small repairs done, but the agent whose services we tried to enlist did not appear and at one time it looked as though we would fail altogether, until we had the good fortune to receive a call from Captain Georges Jochumsen, a former Norwegian sailing-ship master who recently started a ship chandlery on the Vieux Port. Captain Jochumsen was the soul of helpfulness.

We sailed next morning for Sète, intending to arrive there that evening, but on passage a gale warning for the area came over the R/T, so we altered course and put into Port de Bouc, not an attractive place for a yacht, but cheerfully unpretentious and full of Scandinavian tanker crews not averse to alcoholic intake.

Weather improved next day enough for us to make Sète by hugging the shore to avoid the full effects of the north-west winds. As we approached, the wind dropped and the sun shone a farewell benediction to the Middle Sea. We made fast at the canal quay close to the Customs House and I went off in search of fresh water. This involved a tremendous process. Although there was a mains connection alongside, it could be opened only by a waterman from the Mairie. This gentleman was eventually located, we washed decks and filled up with the most expensive water I have ever shipped—10 minutes of it cost me Frs 759.

Next day we successfully finished the unpleasant tasks of removing deck gear and davits—long sealed with paint and rust—and I made some inquiries of the local Ponts et Chaussées office about the canals before us. They were polite, but were not able to help us much.

We had room for a little fuel and I went alongside and filled up. The price was about right—Frs 22 a litre—and we were told that, since we were getting it at duty-free prices prior to an inland voyage, we would be inspected on arrival at Bordeaux and charged duty on what we would have used. I learned that, as we could fill up in the canal at much the same price, we might well reach Bordeaux with an apparently almost nil consumption, so that all this solemn farce was useless, but as obviously no one was taking it seriously anyway, we found it best simply to comply and say nothing. We duly furnished ourselves with a Customs entry permit after some delay.

After preparing ourselves, both documentarily and practically, for the canals, we found out that, in order to get into the Etang de Thau, the lake leading to the canal proper, we would have to pass beneath no fewer than five bridges, all of which would either rise or swing for us. As one was a railway bridge, we could only pass at certain times of the day, which meant that, in fact, there were only two periods when all could be negotiated without waiting. This involved leaving our berth either at 0700 or at 1545 hours. We chose the latter but, even so, had some trouble stemming the current as we waited for each bridge to open. This current depends on the direction of recent winds: when they have been easterly, it sweeps from the sea into the Etang de Thau, and when westerly, it rushes out. It is almost never still.

After spending the night just inside the Etang de Thau and having a chat with another British yacht, Mr James Byrnes's 47-ton *Shrimp*, which was preparing to winter in Sète, we sailed next morning across the Etang in brilliant sunshine. The pilot book gives no directions and no charts are available. On leaving the red beacon tower to port, steer generally WSW 'towards the mountain', so the myriad fishermen told us, and eventually steer for the red-and-white lighthouse tower marking Les Onglous, the hamlet at the entry to the canal. The channel is not buoyed, but this approximate course caused my echo-sounder to give depths of 25–30 ft near Sète and eventually 10–12 ft near Les Onglous. The red-and-black-lit beacon tower ahead of you on leaving Sète should be left to starboard. A good mark for yachts sailing in the opposite direction might be the single tall factory chimney near Sète, to be kept fine on the starboard bow while crossing the Etang.

After two locks and some lengthy pounds, the canal debouches into the River Hérault. We sailed merrily downstream with the current almost into the town of Agde until—to our horror—we saw a weir ahead. There was absolutely nothing to indicate that it was coming or where we should, in fact, have turned to starboard into another canal cutting. Both motors hard astern enabled us to avoid disaster and enter the cutting leading to the notorious round lock of Agde. It has three gates, one in the direction whence we came, one in the direction in which we were going and a third leading away into the River Hérault and seldom used. Here we came face to face with the bridge we had heard about back in Cannes, and indeed it looked exceptionally low. The lock-keepers shouted at us not to be afraid; so I carried on, only to find that my heating chimney and loud-hailer both stuck under it. So we spent a while removing them before ultimately we carried on and passed beneath it, triumphant in the knowledge that henceforth we could safely pass under anything that showed itself.

After Agde there are some long straight pounds and Bureaux de Déclarations (control posts) are frequent at the few locks encountered. Navigation finishes at 1800 in the autumn and we made Béziers Port just in time. The town is attractive, but the canal port is too far from it for convenience. Officials told us that there was no point in trying to go farther that night, as the celebrated flight of the Seven Locks, a few kilometres beyond, was reserved next morning from 0600 to 0900 for downcoming traffic and we would not be allowed to go up until after then.

Indeed, next morning we had to wait nearly an hour at the foot of the Seven Locks before downcoming traffic was through and the two barges ahead of us had started their slow progress uphill through the (thank heaven) electrically operated locks. Here a plaque commemorates the conception and building of the Canal du Midi by Paul Riquet in the seventeenth century.

The Seven Locks are followed by the Malpas Tunnel—only a very short affair—and a pound no less than 54 km. in length, but often very twisting, so that we now and then had to make two bites at a corner and went in constant fear of meeting a barge at an awkward moment on a bend. Some of the turns in this part of the canal are as much as 180 degrees, so that one appears to be going in the reverse direction, and no amount of pretty scenery in this lovely wine district of France can atone for the constant anxiety felt. Traffic was mercifully light: the Ponts et Chaussées at Toulouse later told us that it seldom exceeded fifty vessels a week in each direction.

Navigation on the Canal du Midi as a whole was the most difficult I have ever experienced in all my years of 'ditch-crawling' in France, Belgium, Netherlands, Germany and Sweden. This is due, apart from the extreme sinuosity of the canal, to its shallow depth and the fact that the sides are improperly dredged, making turning at bends especially difficult and causing frequent troubles when you have to pull in to the sides to avoid hitting a barge. For instance, when we arrived at a lovely little wine village called Homps that night, we made in all innocence for the side of the widened canal known as the 'port', only to find ourselves fast in the mud. A tractor and the entire village helped get us off. The café proprietor told me that it was five years since this part was last dredged and vessels often got stuck here.

Next day being Sunday, there was a marked increase in traffic, mostly consisting of petrol barges returning light from Toulouse to the refineries on the Etang de Thau. A strong wind made waiting to enter the locks difficult: the locks themselves on the Canal du Midi are oval in shape instead of being rectangular. Goodness knows why Riquet ever built them like this; perhaps the barges of those days fitted them more easily. The effect now is for a vessel to move unduly while the lock is filling, as it is impossible to keep her close to the sides. Many of the locks were double, or even treble. The system is for them to be filled two at a time; the vessel moves forward into the next lock and the gate is closed astern of her before filling the third lock. We made fast close to Carcassonne railway station just as dusk was falling.

Carcassonne is a city that cannot be ignored, so the next forenoon was spent in sightseeing. The sunlit afternoon, however, saw us again on our way. We had noticed that the lock-keepers always stood to receive us on the side of the lock opposite to the bollards. This was particularly annoying, as they were thus unable to help make fast and valuable time was lost while we climbed ashore to do so. At length we were goaded into asking why this was, to which we received the reply that it was the business of the 'marin' (seaman) in the barges to leap ashore with the warps, the lock-keepers 'not being paid' to help boats make fast—only to open and close gates. This curious attitude persisted the whole length of the Canal du Midi, where the keepers were generally aged, inefficient and unimaginative. They also had little idea of how to treat a small craft and used always to let the water into their locks both too soon and too fast, so that we did ourselves much needless damage. However, after Toulouse things improved considerably.

We passed the summit level, where the canal is alimented by a small rivulet from the adjacent Montagnes Noires and were thankfully and at long last going downhill. As in the main canals in the centre of France, the Canal du Midi has a summit level at each end of which is a lock; they are known respectively as Ecluse de la Mediterranée and Ecluse de l'Ocean. A new era was breaking. The height of the summit-level above sea-level is 188.43 m. (about 618 ft) and the source of the alimentary stream is 65 km. distant.

Our arrival in Toulouse caused something of a sensation, as it coincided with the rush hour while we were passing through the curious Bayard Lock opposite the railway station. This lock is actually placed beneath a road bridge and a crowd often gathers to watch the ordeals of those in the boat below. The lock was the most difficult since Agde and we had to remove our ensign staff to prevent it breaking. We finally berthed in a wide basin which is the meeting-point of the Canal du Midi, with which we were now finished, the Canal Latéral à la Garonne and two small alimentary canals leading into the River Garonne. We watered from a convenient 'bistro' and could have fuelled if we had wished. The place was known as 'Les Ponts Jumeaux' (the twin bridges) and was a 10-minute bus ride from the town centre. We were royally received by M. Michel Petitjean, who was, we discovered to our surprise and delight, commodore of the Yacht Club de Toulouse.

Here Douglas, our cook, had to leave to go back to London, so that Arthur, my hand, and myself were left in sole occupation of the yacht. At first I wondered how this was going to work out, but we soon found that, as all the locks were now descending and as the Canal Latéral à la Garonne was so much deeper, straighter and more modern than the picturesque Midi, things were quite easy for just the two of us.

In Toulouse, I visited the Ponts et Chaussées office, which proved a mine of valuable information about the canal and which rendered me a great service in fetching a boathook that we had left behind at a lock the previous day. Everywhere along the canal, in fact, people were the soul of friendliness and help.

The Toulouse Ponts et Chaussées gave me much material about the canal which has probably not been made public to tourists to date. It seemed to me a pity that this material, all of great use to tourists and to yachtsmen in particular, should be kept at the bottom of a drawer in an office in Toulouse, whereas surely it should be made available to tourist bureaux and to bookshops. Everywhere in France the dead hand of officialdom seems to strangle its own enterprise: guide-books and maps are published at great expense for the public service and are seldom if ever on sale to the public itself. Even the French official handbook to their own inland waterways, brought up to date and reissued in 1958, is unobtainable except in Paris and Marseille.

After a day's rest in Toulouse we started off on our attack on the Canal Latéral à la Garonne. This proved a very different matter. Apart from a slight 'contretemps' with a bargee whose moorings we had broken by going too fast past his moored barge (quickly settled by a cash payment), there were no untoward events. We never once grounded, there were no 180-degree turns and there were bollards on each side of every lock. The canal lock-keepers seemed less decrepit and more numerous. An official from Toulouse drove up to assure us that the broken warp incident was closed. The sun shone. Everyone seemed happy. Even the bridges were higher and wider.

After passing twenty-three locks, we found ourselves over the Pont-Canal across the River Tarn, but still three locks short of the picturesque old town of Moissac, where we had intended spending the night. Navigation was officially over, but the lock-keepers were extraordinarily helpful and telephoned the local engineer-in-chief to get his permission to let us lock through into the town, where we were able to spend the night comfortably.

Next morning I was a little surprised to be summoned by a policeman to accompany him to the police station with all our papers. On arrival, I found that a photograph I had taken the previous day of a petrol tank by the canal had been viewed with suspicion by some bargee or other, who had raised a hue and cry after me. It was at the time of some of the later Algerian troubles and I suspect that our furled Red Ensign had been mistaken either for the Red Flag or something equally sinister. Needless to say, the incident was good-humouredly disposed of. Moissac has a lovely abbey, of which I was able to get some (quite legitimate, I hope) shots.

The next day but one was almost our last in the canal and we managed to reach Meilhan, a charming village only 18 km. from the point where the canal joins the River Garonne at Castets. By now we were very expert at locking through and some fast times were being recorded. Our fastest time locking through (bow in to bow out) was just under 4 minutes. Sometimes the approach to a lock was made difficult by a drainage sluice to one side or the other causing a current which took us over just as we were making our approach, but we learned to expect this and take it into account.

On October 20 we rose early, meaning to lock through out of the canal as soon as possible and stem the tide in the River Garonne down to Bordeaux.

When we arrived at Castets the lock-keeper asked us whether we wished to wait with the barges already there or carry straight on. I replied that we would go straight on and a barge was moved out of the lock so that we could use it, but on arrival in the lock the other bargees began strongly to advise us to await at least half-tide with them and then to go down the river in convoy. They said it was dangerous to go alone and, in face of all this advice, I changed my mind and agreed. A fellow came up and offered to pilot us down for Frs 3,000, but it was now clearly unnecessary.

We had arrived at Castets Lock at 1000 hours and at 1200 hours we locked through into the Garonne. It was a wonderful sensation, after the frustrations of so much canal life, to be in the freedom of a wide river. We obediently followed the barges, but later on, when my depth-sounder showed 25 ft below us, we went ahead of them. I later regretted this, as the sounder later showed very much less water and I was worried that we were not in the proper channel. However, we soon sighted the Pont de Pierre ahead of us and knew we were nearing Bordeaux. The river water, deep green in the higher reaches, had changed its colour to a yellowy brown which was very unattractive. We passed beneath the Pont de Pierre, the old stone bridge which marks the division between the maritime and riverine sections of Bordeaux Port, 4 hours after leaving the canal. To our

great delight, H.M.S. *Birmingham* was lying alongside one of the quays and
we managed to get permission to berth alongside her, thus avoiding tending our warps all night in the considerable rise and fall.

We had been under more or less continuous way for just 8½ days between
Sète and Bordeaux, a distance of 510 km. (around 320 miles), had negotiated 152 locks and thoroughly enjoyed ourselves.

Bordeaux was a very much nicer town than we had expected. It is full
of splendid buildings, broad streets and ancient curiosities. The food is
excellent and the inhabitants traditionally courteous and kind to the
British, to whom they are linked by the centuries-old bonds of the wine
trade. It is thus worth more than a brief visit.

From a yachtsman's point of view, however, it has the great dis-
advantage that there is nowhere convenient for a yacht to lie within the
city centre. As soon as H.M.S. *Birmingham* sailed we found ourselves alongside the river quay, coping with a very large rise and fall and with a swift
and muddy current. We accordingly shifted berth that same day into the
Bacalan Basin No. 1, locking through near high water around midday.
The lock gates are conveniently placed at a point where the current is
lessened by a bend in the river, but there is usually a long wait while the
ponderous gates are prepared. Once in the basin, of which there are several,
we felt very unhappy, as the situation was extremely dirty. Fresh water was
available, but only by means of the fire brigade and a terrible to-do with
hose-pipes. We did, however, make use of our new-found tranquillity by
getting into touch with a local shipyard, Messrs G. Mounerat et F.
Gaussens, who were extremely helpful in organizing our running repairs.

The basin was several miles from the centre of the city, so that we thankfully accepted Messrs Mounerat's suggestion to return farther upriver to
M. A. Bugaret's hospitable riverside shipyard, where at low water we dried
sufficiently for the repairs to the rudder to be done. This was not altogether
an easy operation, due to the run of current, the angle at which the pontoon
lay at low water and the muddy bottom on which to work, but the men
concerned found a way in which to do everything and indeed appeared to
be thoroughly enjoying the unusual job of tending a yacht in Bordeaux.

While this was going on we did a certain amount of sightseeing, had
some laundry done and recharged the gas bottles. I also went along to pay
our dues for having locked in and out of the Bacalan Basin the previous day.

Early on the morning of October 24 we made some trials and, these
being as satisfactory as seemed possible, put our yard party ashore and set
course downriver. The sun was shining brightly and visibility was excellent.
I had heard much about fog in the Gironde, so we were glad to have a good
day on which to make a start into the Atlantic. Years of Mediterranean
cruising had made me a little nervous of coming back to the Bay, especially
through the medium of a crowded commercial river, but with the excellent
Admiralty chart and the good weather, Fate seemed to be playing into our
hands.

In the Gironde the tide ebbs for 8 hours and flows for 4, so that we
reckoned that, although our trials had caused us to miss a good deal of the
first ebb, we could get at least to Pauillac, 26 miles downriver, before the
flood. A couple of miles down the Gironde, to port, we passed Point du
Jour, where the Bordeaux Yacht Club has its H.Q. and a lot of people
waved to us from the boats. Arthur Walker, who was to be my crew for
the whole trip home, was delighted to be under way again and so was
I.

The Gironde, a filthy muddy brown for its entire length, was extremely
well buoyed, although, as so often happens, the characteristics and mark-
ings of the buoys did not always tally exactly with our Admiralty chart.
This was very noticeable at Bec d'Ambès, the place where the river
Dordogne flows into the Gironde and where the marking system is complicated. For instance, one of the principal buoys marked on the chart as
BA and coloured black was found, in fact, to be marked BAO and to be
painted bright red. This may have been due to the recent wreck of a
medium-sized Dutch freighter, which was encumbering the river at this
point, pending salvage.

Our friends in Bordeaux had told us that we could well make fast at the
river pilots' berth at Pauillac for the night and interest ourselves by
sampling the famous wines from this part of the world, but when we
arrived off Pauillac, just as the flood was beginning to make, the pilots
assured us that this would not be allowed, and so, not relishing more warp
trouble during the night and being anxious to profit from the fine weather,
we decided to push on against the flood to Royan at the mouth of the river.
We were very glad to have taken this decision, for the adverse effect of the
tide proved very much less than we had expected and we arrived off Royan

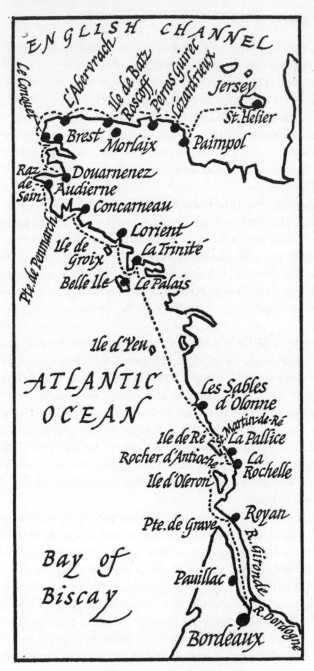

11. Bordeaux to Jersey by the Bay

—more or less at H.W.—at 1615, having made the passage from Bordeaux in just over 7 hours in perfect conditions.

Our visit to Royan was short. For the locals quickly told us that we would dry out at half-tide everywhere and, as we planned sailing at low water next morning to carry us north to La Rochelle, this would be extremely inconvenient. We therefore decided to steam the 3 to 4 miles across the estuary to the small deep-water port of Port Bloc on the southern side. On the Admiralty chart, this is referred to as Pointe de Grave, which is, in fact, the local name for the cape adjacent. The main run of the tide and river is just off the harbour entrance, so that due allowance has to be made for what sometimes amounts to a 4-knot current before sheltered water is reached.

Port Bloc is about the least interesting port I have ever visited, but it is splendidly accessible at all states of the tide and perfectly clean. The little town is about 3 miles away and we were lucky to find a car to give us a lift to do the day's shopping, because there are no shops at the harbour at all.

Next morning we sailed at 0800—low water—picking our way rather nervously through the morning mists from buoy to barely visible buoy. The approaches to the Gironde are excellently marked and nothing need go wrong if only the channel is followed carefully. But if you are so rash as to steer north of the channel before you are well outside it you will risk going aground on the sandbanks which line it. The cruel sea breaks mercilessly on them. *En route* seawards we spoke on the R/T to the shore station at Bordeaux-Arcachon and later to the Gironde pilot vessel, still lurking off Royan. Several large vessels were waiting outside for the tide. We set course northwards up the French Atlantic coast without going right out to the landfall buoy, as there was plenty of water and a short cut seemed fully justified. Again the chart proved wrong as to detail, showing a wreck buoy as green/red, whereas it was, in fact, plain green. There was no wind, the sea was flat calm and visibility rather poor.

I had cherished the idea of taking the tortuous and obviously very interesting channel inside Ile d'Oleron, but the experts had advised strongly against it. We therefore took the tide northwards outside Oleron, which was barely distinguishable in the haze, until the important lighthouse on Pointe de Chassiron came up, shortly followed by the Rocher d'Antioche surrounded by broken water. The Biscay pilot did its best to cause confusion by referring to the Rocher beacon as being painted red, whereas it was black and white. Here we altered course 070 degrees to steer for La Rochelle and were met by a number of local trawlers on a reciprocal course.

Less than an hour later the spectacular skyline of medieval La Rochelle came into view and it was not long afterwards that we found ourselves steaming between the twin towers of St Nicholas and La Chaine into the outer harbour at high water. There was a slight delay while the gang that opens the lock gates and bridge leading into the inner basin was fetched, after which we dropped the hook and went astern to the quay and had our first real fresh-water scrub-down for several weeks.

We were six days in this hospitable harbour cleaning off the canal dirt and doing some repainting and varnishing in perfect October weather. The Commodore and officers of the Société des Régates de La Rochelle came aboard and we exchanged burgees, later visiting their unique clubhouse in the Tour de la Chaine. Repairs were easy and not too expensive and I went on the grid to change my propellers and scrape the bottom. One dynamo was sent to Paris to be rewound.

There is just time, by leaving La Rochelle as soon as the lock gates open, to make the picturesque port of St Martin-de-Ré on the Ile de Ré opposite before the St Martin lock gates close on the same tide. The distance is about 12 miles, so one has to step on it. To make doubly sure, I had telephoned the St Martin lock-keeper to warn him of our arrival. Almost everyone in La Rochelle was assembled at the basin to bid us farewell, and our discomfiture had to be seen to be believed when, after a few plaintive puffs, both diesels stalled. We had somehow or other turned off the fuel during repairs and forgotten to turn it on again. It took 40 minutes to persuade them to start and in this time we had obviously missed our tide. Not to start would, however, have been too much of an anticlimax, so sail we did. But as soon as we were around the corner, instead of continuing hopelessly towards St Martin in the gathering dusk, I put into the busy commercial port of La Pallice five miles away and spent a horrible night among discharging freighters and groaning cranes.

But next morning we did actually get to St Martin and I hastened to make my apologies to the lock-keeper for the mishaps of the previous day. We did not lock in, and merely stayed an hour or so in the slowly drying outer harbour. On leaving, we made rendezvous with two sailing yachts from La Rochelle who had planned a week-end in Sables d'Olonne, our next port of call some 30 miles northward. We kept company with them for a while, but absence of wind made progress so slow that we eventually left them. On passage, we had our first taste of the long Atlantic rollers and made Les Sables d'Olonne soon after lunch.

Les Sables d'Olonne is a depressing but amiable sort of place. The harbour has plenty of water at all states of the tide, but there is almost nowhere for a yacht to lie except outboard of a herd of fishing-vessels, which seem to delight in sailing at all hours of the night. Fuel and fresh water are available at a filthily dirty quay next to what seems to be a main drain. But everyone is cheerful and nice, although I must confess that All Saints spent in a deserted French holiday resort in drenching rain and a high wind is not my idea of real fun. But what Les Sables lacked as a yacht harbour it amply atoned for in delightful people and we did not regret our two days of enforced idleness while the winds dropped.

Trawler activity during the ensuing night clearly indicated that the weather had improved and we managed to sail early next morning on the 80-mile leg from Les Sables to Belle Ile (Le Palais). Though there was considerable swell all day, except inside Ile d'Yeu, the sea surface was smooth and progress was rapid. It was found difficult to know how much leeway to allow for the tide, which in these parts set off the shore seawards at rates impossible to estimate. Nevertheless, each buoy was picked up with reasonable accuracy, and the small port of Le Palais on the landward side of Belle Ile was eventually made soon after dark. Here we lay alongside a fisherman in the outer harbour until the basin opened.

The furious winds next morning gave us the necessary excuse to spend the day touring Belle Ile, and there was no trouble in hiring a self-drive car in which to do so. Even next morning, many of the locals were still of the opinion that we ought not to sail, although we were only bound so far as La Trinité-sur-Mer, 18 miles eastward. There is a local passage known as La Teigneuse which is greatly feared and this figured largely in the discussion. I was nevertheless certain that we could make it easily. The Teigneuse passage, when we came to it, proved no trouble at all and we went alongside the quay in the delightful harbour of La Trinité-sur-Mer some 2½ hours later. This is the best natural harbour on this coast that I have visited, being quite sheltered from all winds and always having plenty of water. Dr Alain Bombard's new yacht was there, looking very smart. A very hospitable local fellow took us for a motor drive through the celebrated Stones of Carnac, which we had, in fact, come there to see; and memories of the Battle of Quiberon Bay were also revived.

Next day's passage to Lorient was far less pleasant: the sea was rough and on the port bow all the way, while visibility was poor, Ile de Groix only turning up at the last minute. I was thankful to go alongside an out-of-commission trawler in Lorient, where I thought the police and Immigration made an unnecessary fuss about us, presumably because it was a naval base. But the presence aboard of our French host of the motor drive at Carnac gave us respectability and the formalities were quickly over. Although good for stores, Lorient is about the most depressing port I know in this part of the world and the town entirely lacks character. I advise yachtsmen against it.

Our next port—Concarneau—two days later, was quite a different matter. This place is so well known to British yachts that one hesitates to embark afresh on its praises. I can, however, personally vouch that that November it was at its best, being bathed in hot sunshine and looking extremely lovely. Even the fish seemed less offensive than elsewhere. Most yachts, we were told, usually lay at anchor in the outer harbour, but we went alongside in the inner harbour and suffered no inconvenience other than that the high spring tide put us on the mud just before sailing-time, so that we stayed longer than we meant. While there, we took a bus drive to Quimper and among other things inspected the berth in the River Odet, where a yacht can lie if she makes the lovely river trip up from Benodet at the mouth. I have heard this described as the most beautiful river trip in France.

We found the leg from Concarneau to Pointe de Penmarch, where the English Channel officially begins, a little tricky at first, due to the immense number of islets comprising the Iles des Glénans, so that some careful navigation was necessary. But the passage off the redoubtable Pointe de Penmarch itself was effected in the nearest possible local approach to a flat calm. On rounding the point, I altered course eastward and in the excellent visibility far off we could see the Pointe du Raz and off it the most serious danger we anticipated this trip—the infamous Raz de Sein. We were making such good progress that I almost felt tempted to pass the Raz de Sein that evening, but it was springs and the tide would be adverse, so discretion triumphed and at 1645 I dropped the hook in a small cove known as the Anse de Ste Evette, off Audierne, inside the Pointe du Raz. Here in recent times a breakwater a couple of cables in length had been built to create an artificial deep-water harbour for vessels not wishing to dry out upriver at the port of Audierne. At its seaward end was a fixed red light. None of this was shown on the chart. During the night it came on to blow and we awoke to find ourselves swinging all over the harbour.

The berth off Audierne was, in fact, so unpleasant that we decided at all costs to leave next day, even if the race should engulf us. And so at 1000, an hour which I had calculated as reasonable for the passage, we weighed and were about to leave the anchorage when the fisherman alongside implored us to await the afternoon tide and sail with him. He added that we were then too late for the tide and, if we insisted on sailing then, we would find a strong north-going tide running against the Force 4–5 NW. wind and would surely have a very uncomfortable time. He also offered us a pilot, whom we embarked forthwith. We felt much happier.

And so at 1430 we weighed again and followed our fishermen friends out to sea. There was some swell, but nothing very serious. By 1540 we had La Vieille lighthouse a cable or so on our starboard beam and began to alter course around the Pointe du Raz. I was pleased to note the ferry launch from the Ile de Sein, which at least showed that the experts were at one in reckoning this the most favourable moment. The sea here altered in character and considerable broken water was met, the waves seeming to come from every direction. We slavishly followed our fishing boat—appropriately named *Marchons Ensemble*. On rounding La Vieille and the lit beacon just outside it, the fisherman altered course to starboard and I found to my delight that this landed us in a relatively calm stretch of water. My pleasure was not to last long, however, for conditions soon became confused again and, in fact, remained so until we had rounded Basse Jaune buoy half an hour later and set course 085 degrees for Douarnenez. Generally speaking, I would describe the passage of the Raz de Sein as less arduous and certainly less lengthy than that of the Race of Alderney (Raz Blanchard), although it can have its moments of concentrated unpleasantness. Taken as we did it, it can be regarded as operative in two sections, one off La Vieille lighthouse and another off the Pointe du Van (northern end of Baie des Trépassés) with a stretch of relative calm in between.

The approach to Douarnenez is curious at night, due to the absence of leading lights. It is not until the very last moment that the occulting white light on the head of one of the two breakwaters becomes visible. There is only one quay—very fishy—where one does not dry out. Despite all the publicity it has received, the town struck us as uninteresting, with shops miles from the harbour. We lay alongside a sardine boat bound for Morocco.

Douarnenez–Brest, performed two days later in near-fog conditions, was not really a necessary journey, as we could have continued through the Chenal du Four and given Brest a miss. But as we had never been there, we liked the thought of seeing the great French naval base. Nor were we disappointed, for at their moorings in the military port lay the battleship *Richelieu*, the cruiser *Jeanne d'Arc* and a host of other famous names. We made fast alongside a dredger in the commercial harbour, which was unexpectedly clean, and spent a quiet night. We were examined only perfunctorily.

Fog enshrouded Brest Roads next morning, but we were told that conditions seaward were better, so we sailed and soon found that this was so. Visibility, in fact, became good and we were favoured with a flat calm as we passed down the majestic Brest approaches towards the Vieux Moines beacon some 13 miles distant. It is here that the Chenal du Four, one of the two channels inshore of Ushant, begins. The channel itself is extremely well marked and we had no qualms at all as we passed northwards along it, sighting Le Conquet on our starboard hand and recalling memories of many radio chats with this well-known French station.

The coast to starboard became increasingly rocky and dangerous, reminiscent of so much of northern Brittany, and we remembered that we were at last entering home waters. Before sunset, we made L'Abervrach and anchored for the night off the village, where the inhabitants, it being out of season, insisted on organizing some gyrations which they described as 'Breton folk dances'. Everyone was very, very jolly.

Despite an adverse tide the whole way from L'Abervrach to Ile de Batz, we managed to sight Roscoff by 1430 and I started to make a very cautious low-water approach. Unfortunately, however, I had no large-scale chart of the approaches aboard, so that it soon became obvious we could not make it safely. I accordingly altered course to circumnavigate Ile de Batz and made the standard southerly approach to Morlaix Roads, of which I had a large-scale chart. Even so, the dangers looked formidable. I had to get to Morlaix to collect some mail, so I decided to push as far upriver as was possible, although it was still pretty close to low water. As expected, we were soon aground, but the flood set in and we were eventually able to make a crab-like progress up the river in the dark. It being Sunday, there was nobody manning the locks, so someone had to be chased out before we could get into the harbour, where we eventually made fast at 2030. Our berth was just opposite Dr Pillet's hospitable house. He is the Commodore of the Morlaix Yacht Club and was of the greatest help to us during our two-day visit, which included a motor drive with the Pillets through some of the local sights.

It was already November 18 and quite late enough in the season. We sailed from Morlaix in rather poor visibility and conditions on our run along the Brittany coast towards Lézardrieux became poorer all the time. Tolerable as far as Pérros Guirec, they then worsened steadily, so that our final approach to Lézardrieux River with wind against tide was about the worst moment in our whole trip up the Bay. When at long last the leading lights finally came into line, we were very greatly relieved. Navigation in these inshore waters in the dark is no pleasure, however well one knows them, especially when fog is in the offing.

A night in Lézardrieux to recover, a night in Paimpol basin to touch up our topsides, and we set off on the last leg of our 1,000-mile journey from Cannes to Jersey. But it was not to be. The notoriously bad conditions in the Bréhat approach channel when the tide is ebbing against a fresh NE. wind made things so miserable that we returned to Lézardrieux for a final wait. Not until two days later, on November 23, did we finally head out of Brittany homeward-bound. Friendly Barnouic Tower came up and soon after lunch, with only a moderate sea running, I was able to give my E.T.A. to Jersey Radio. La Corbière, Noirmont, the old familiar marks came flooding back to me, and at 1700 on the dot, we honoured our E.T.A. by passing St Helier pierheads. We had completed 1,085 sea-miles since leaving Cannes on October 2 via Sète-Bordeaux and we were both very glad to be home.

4

Through the Iron Curtain

'September Tide' accepts an invitation to Eastern Germany and Poland

In January 1959 I decided that I would take my boat behind the Iron Curtain. No one from Britain had, so far as I knew, done this since the war. I had heard of the Marconi experimental yacht, *Elettra II*, going to Gdynia; but I could find no trace of a genuine pleasure yacht from these shores ever having been farther east in the Baltic than Travemünde—the last West German port.

And so I started on the round of offices that I thought might help me. First call, naturally, was the Polish Consulate-General in London. I was received courteously, if a trifle impersonally, and was told that my only hope of getting the necessary visa was for the secretary of my yacht club to write to the Polish Yachting Association and get me 'invited'. So I obediently applied to the secretary of the Royal Thames, the senior yacht club I belong to, and he obligingly wrote off to the address in Warsaw which the Poles had given us.

The months passed. No reply from Warsaw. The Polish Consulate also wrote—they even telephoned—still no reply. Meanwhile, I had found myself in East Berlin, where I had gone to a lot of trouble to visit what I was told was the equivalent of a Foreign Office, had myself photographed at some expense, filled in several forms in triplicate and finally handed the whole thing over to a grim-looking woman who told me that I 'would be advised later'. And so I had applied also for an East German visa.

I came back to London. Still no reply from the Poles, despite several more letters from us. At length, I mentioned the matter casually to Francis

Usborne, secretary of the Royal Yachting Association, and asked him if he would like to have a try. He did, in fact, try with such effect that within two days he had had a telephone call from Warsaw, which said my visa would be granted at once, and I also had a welcoming letter from the East German Yachting Association saying that they would be delighted to see me there at any time and that my visa was on the way. It was already April and by some curious chance the mail that brought my letter of invitation—with assurance of visa—from the East Germans also delivered me a blunt refusal from the East German Foreign Ministry. A few days later I was officially advised from both countries and the cat seemed in the bag.

So far as Eastern Germany was concerned, there were no further visa troubles, for the authority to enter the country had duly arrived. I was even sent some East German charts—later to prove quite invaluable—and given details of fuelling, etc. The Poles were much less efficient. Apparently, their London Consulate was not allowed to issue the visa until 15 days before I entered the country, and all efforts of mine to point out that—as the visa did not become valid until July 1, and I wanted to sail in May—I would thus be forced to return to London at great expense seemed to mean nothing to them. As in most satellite countries, no one will ever take any responsibility, especially where no precedent exists. It was not until I had persuaded the Polish Ambassador to London to intervene for me that things began to make sense.

In fact, at many points in the long months of waiting and irritating delay trying to get both Polish and East German visas, I was on the point of abandoning the whole business. Officialdom everywhere is often maddening, but in the Eastern 'bloc' it is worse than elsewhere. I could not help laughing when, finally, the Polish Ambassador told me that, as my crew and I would be living aboard our ship during all our visit to Poland, we could have been treated as merchant seamen and no visas were therefore required. His consulate had never mentioned this to me. Nevertheless, despite the Ambassador's excellent suggestion, I got the visa stamped in our passports and, pale but triumphant, sailed from Jersey, my home port, on May 11.

It was ideal weather—windless, with fair visibility and flat calm. So it was the more annoying when, due to trouble in one engine, I found myself unable to stem the strong tide in the Race of Alderney. After some hours without apparently making the least headway, we finally managed to reach Braye Harbour, Alderney, where the repairs were made and we spent the night.

Ideal weather again greeted us next day and we had a delightful and uneventful passage to the Hamble. The inevitable visit to the Bugle Inn followed and all hands were at their best next morning, when our peace was shattered by the British Customs. I have sailed boats to many countries and always, in my experience, it is our own Customs fellows who are the most troublesome. These men were no exception. Apart from having to count every bottle and every cigarette, we were forced to fill in endless forms swearing that we were not importing the yacht for more than a certain time. One hears so many complaints from yachtsmen of what they suffer at the hands of British Customs—and yet no one ever seems to lift a finger in self-defence. Why yachtsmen should always be treated as criminals, especially in their own country, is a thing I have never been able to understand. At last, to everyone's relief, they were gone and we were able to settle down to breakfast.*

From the Hamble to Newhaven was an easy run. The Customs man at Hamble had told me to hoist a Red Ensign at the yard and tie a knot in it on arriving at Newhaven. This, he said, meant 'I am carrying dutiable stores and I do not require Customs'. Both statements were certainly true. I only wished that Customs had understood it. It was a new one on me, too. For the privilege of spending one night alongside a dirty berth in Newhaven we were charged a little over 21s. The man who issued the receipt on behalf of British Railways told me, what I could well believe, that everyone complained and nobody did anything about it. If I had had the energy, I would have written to the R.Y.A. and the local yacht club, but of course I never put pen to paper.

Newhaven to Dover; Dover to Ostend (the North Sea Yacht Club is first-class and the officials more accommodating than our own, but the harbour needed dredging at low water). Ostend to Flushing on a wild sunlit day with the spring tide flooding up the Scheldt against a north-easter. Not so funny; we should have kept closer inshore, as the Ostend pilot had said.

Flushing to Rotterdam and its excellent De Maas Yacht Club. The

*Let's face it—they have improved a lot since then.

17. Warnemünde. The inner harbour.

18. Stralsund. The lovely silhouette of this old Hansa town.

19. These two men, customs and police, came aboard *September Tide* to clear her when she left East Germany. Note their launch astern.

20. The Polish Navy at Sunday Church Parade at Swinoujscje.

21. Regatta at Swinoujscje 18–25 June 1959.

22. Kolberg. The
sandy coastline looking
east.

23. Looking towards the Russian frontier. The tower that Copernicus built at Frombork.

24. Looking into the Vistula at Przegalina.

engineers found I had a warp around one propeller—obviously picked up manoeuvring at Ostend at low water—and we went into dry dock to take it off. It was a curious dock: the ship entered it stern first, some underwater contraption rose and hoisted our stern out of the water. I thought all our deck gear would slide overboard, but nothing happened.

12. From Jersey to Holland

From Rotterdam through Leyden and Amsterdam and the Ijssel Meer (why will people still call it the Zuyder Zee?) and the great North Holland Canal to Delfzijl. And so we left the Netherlands.

It was blowing a bit, so I decided against going down the Ems Estuary with the tide to Borkum and then out to sea. Instead, we picked our way from buoy to buoy across the treacherous 'Watt' inside the Friesians. Thank goodness we had brought the local German charts in Delfzijl, for the Admiralty charts of these waters were quite useless. In fact, it was our experience on the whole of this trip that, at least for a yacht, Admiralty charts (except, of course, for passage) cease to have any value when you leave the British coastline. True, they make few actual mistakes, but the vast majority of the buoys that a yacht would normally have to make inshore are simply not marked. The only reliable charts are those of the country in whose waters you find yourself.

It was a neap tide over the sands. Foolhardy by nature, I once cut a corner and the boat touched bottom. Horrified, we put about into deeper water. No damage was done. I blessed the echo-sounder and the new oil-filled transducer which Pye had sent me. It gave me *accurate readings* down to some 2 ft—an essential in these parts. The worst hazard was the shallow patch just off Norddeich radio station. The echo-sounder registered 3 ft, then 2, then seemed to give up altogether. We held our breath. The

sounder again showed 2, 3, 4, 6—thank God, we had crossed the Rubicon
and we soon found ourselves in deep water again on our way down to
Norderney. Ten minutes later, and I doubt if we would have made it.

Norderney is not a particularly attractive place to visit in a yacht. The
harbour is some miles from the town and beach and nothing is very pretty
when you get there. But it has the supreme merit of at least being a port of
refuge on an otherwise long and inhospitable coast. Next morning we sailed
at low water to catch the east-going stream into the Elbe. This meant
starting at a moment when there was very little water over the bar to seaward from Norderney, but it being a neap tide, this was just possible with
the echo-sounder registering about 3 ft of water beneath the keel.

It was a lovely run up the swept channel to within sight of the Elbe II
light-vessel, where course was altered to steam up the Elbe on the flood.
Off Cuxhaven, we were hailed by a Customs launch, which asked us where
we were bound. On learning that we were bound for the Kiel Canal and
points north, he asked us to fly the 3rd Substitute flag beneath our ensign.
This indicates 'I am in transit and do not require Customs'.

This signal is more or less standard practice in German waters. There is
no mention of it in the North Sea Pilot Book and more is the pity, for a lot
of anxiety and misunderstanding would be avoided if the Admiralty publications paid more attention to their signals sections. Incidentally, there
was also nothing in the 'pilot' about the numerous pilotage and other
signals made by every merchantman at the mouth of the River Scheldt.
Yachtsmen are often baffled by the absence of information in the Admiralty
pilotage guides about local signals and Customs regulations. Surely this
could be put right.

Locking in at Brunsbüttelkoog, at the southern end of the Kiel Canal,
was fairly quick, for we found the larger of the two locks used already open
and traffic being guided in. We lay astern of a Russian merchantman and
close alongside a West German destroyer (ex-American) known as *Z.1*.
An obliging ship chandler boarded us and took an order for delivery at
the other end of the canal. The representative of the United Baltic Corporation, an Anglo-German company which does yeoman service in looking
after British ships using the canal, also came aboard. The United Baltic
took over all our problems such as canal dues, a berth on arrival in Kiel,
duty-free stores and their payment and the organization of some minor

repairs later. Their customers must surely rise up and call them blessed.

Brunsbüttelkoog has an excellent quiet berth for yachts just inside the lock gates on your port hand going north, where there is also a small yacht club. Here we passed a delightfully peaceful night, serene in the knowledge that henceforth we were finished with tides and all they implied.

The passage of the Kiel Canal next day was fast and easy. We started at 1200 and arrived at 1900. We finally made fast at an excellent berth at the British Kiel Yacht Club at Kiel-Friedrichsort at 2015. The club, which was run by the Royal Engineers, extended the best possible welcome to visitors of all nationalities and did an excellent job in teaching boat-handling to the soldiers of the local British units. We were very glad to be there. The only snag was that it was rather a long way from the town, but, of course, for a one-night stand this was of less importance.

Unfortunately, at Kiel, the German Customs showed a gross in-competence which made us begin to compare them unfavourably even with our own, although they were on the whole more courteous. I had asked for the vessel to be cleared at the southern end of the canal, but there the Customs had assured us this would be better done at the northern end, especially as we were to embark stores in the Kiel Locks. The stores duly came aboard in the locks, but there was no Customs man to clear us. He finally arrived just as we were sitting down to dinner at the yacht club and disorganized the whole evening, remaining aboard until about 2300, counting every bottle and cigarette and painstakingly writing out reams of paper in triplicate. When at length he left he told me that we would be boarded on leaving next day by a Customs launch off Laboe, at the entry to the Kiel Fjord, which would take these papers from us.

It was thus clear that the West German Customs system was less efficient than the British, in that a 'Stores Book' was not issued to visiting yachts, which they could carry around with them as proof of previous German clearance. Accordingly, the whole humiliating and tiresome process of clearing had to be undertaken *de novo* at each port visited. In fact, no Customs launch did board us off Laboe, with the result that, when we arrived at Travemünde next evening, the entire Customs office was thrown into a panic owing to our still having our Kiel papers with us. More of that anon.

The first day of June 1959 was overcast and windless as we made our way up Kiel Fjord to the Kiel lightship before altering course eastwards to coast along, headed for the strait between the mainland and Fehmarn Island. To our annoyance, we were soon approached by a West German patrol launch, which told us that there was to be firing practice from shore batteries that day. We were therefore to keep 8 miles offshore. The Admiralty charts again proved most misleading, as the blue-and-white buoys marking a channel approximately this distance off shore were not marked on them and the usual confusion resulted.

However, the Fehmarn Straits were eventually made and, navigating now on the excellent East German charts which had been sent me, I was able to follow the buoyed channel into Travemünde, which we made in a sudden windstorm at 2100. The East German coast had been plainly visible in the last few hours of the journey and at one point we came close to the Soviet ice-breaker *Krassin*, doing trials in the Bay of Lübeck. I afterwards learned that she had been refitting at Wismar, across the bay in East Germany.

Travemünde is an altogether delightful place for a yacht. The berths in the mouth of the River Trave are excellently arranged alongside the Lübeck Yacht Club, fresh water is laid on; there are many worthy ship chandlers ready to help and there is an efficient small shipyard for any repairs. Add to this the fact that the shops are all mercifully close at hand.

The sight of our Kiel papers still aboard was a mortal blow at the tranquillity of the local Customs, who started the laborious process of counting our stores again from scratch.

The whole trouble with Customs and a smallish yacht (we are 32 tons gross) is that, when one starts on a long foreign trip, the British Customs are kindness itself in allowing the embarkation of enough bonded stores for it. One knows, however, that none of the Scandinavian countries will issue duty-free stores to a yacht, so that one makes sure of taking on, maybe, even more than one may want. The yacht in the early stages of the trip therefore closely resembles a floating wine, tobacco and spirit store and is doubtless liable to excite suspicions on that score.

While in Travemünde for six days prior to our penetration of the Iron Curtain, we had some repairs very well done, repainted ship, took on even more stores and generally prepared ourselves for the unknown. One of the ship chandlers motored us to have a look at the land frontier between West

Germany and the Soviet Zone near Lübeck. It was a grim sight. The former main road from Lübeck to Wismar had been ripped up and in its place was a broad well-raked sand-pit. This pit stretched all along the zonal frontier, which was also guarded by watch-towers, barbed wire and police dogs. The pit was kept well-raked so that footsteps of any wretched refugees trying to escape would at once become apparent. Its macabre lines could be seen stretching all along the frontier formed by the River Trave. On the West German side of the river all was light, bustle and gaiety, but on the East German side there was not a soul to be seen.

Some of the old salts in the harbour started to come aboard and warn me not to go any farther. My Dutch paid hand began to express his doubts, too. One morning he came to me and asked to be signed off. He did not much fancy his chances of safe return. I signed him off and took on a German—a great improvement. I was quite determined to go on.

We didn't feel entirely happy as we slipped from Travemünde. As I finally gave the order to let go I was very conscious that I was severing our last contact with the West. A small crowd of West Germans had assembled to say 'Au revoir', most of them convinced it was 'Adieu'.

John Parkhouse, who had crewed for me before, had arrived that day from London to join. And with us was the faithful and efficient Heinz. It was a lovely day, not a breath of wind, just what a motor boat likes. I had meant to sail the previous day, but we had been delayed and I had sent a telegram—or, at least, paid for one to be sent—to the harbour master at Warnemünde saying we would arrive a day late. There had been some vague reference to an arrival at Warnemünde and it seemed polite to send it. But I was not at all convinced of its arrival.

And so at 0940 on June 7 we cast off. We were in all respects ready for sea and I was determined to make the best possible impression on our Communist hosts. Unfortunately, as we were on course north-east across Lübeck Bay following the buoyed channel, the wind freshened from the north-west and it was not long before the notorious short steep Baltic seas had been whipped up and the yacht's movement became uncomfortable.

Some four hours after sailing, when we had done 26 miles in steadily worsening conditions, we arrived off No. 4 buoy. The Wismar Approach Channel No. 1 buoy was close at hand over to starboard. I accordingly decided to profit from its propinquity and altered course to steer up the first leg of the approach channel. The seas stopped hitting us on the beam and we cleared up some of the debris.

I was at first a little uneasy at this change of plan. Our arrival at Warnemünde would, I supposed, have been more or less expected. But what would the Communists make of our unheralded arrival in Wismar,

13. The East German Coastline

a port we had never even mentioned when discussing our plans? Would we be considered as spies? Smugglers? 'Enemies of the People?' Surely at least as crafty British trying to get the better of the simple proletariat. These thoughts, added to the difficulties of steering a proper course in the rather tortuous approach channel, of which we had not got a proper large-scale chart, made our arrival off Wismar a momentous thing.

We expected to be challenged at any moment, but, surprisingly enough, we had penetrated quite a long way into Wismar Bay before anything happened. We sighted a high-speed launch making for us from the direction of the harbour, which was now plainly visible through the glasses. This launch, packed with youths in sailors' uniforms, circled us (I had, of course, reduced speed) and came alongside, asking who we were. The impact of seeing a smart British motor yacht with colours flying entering an East German harbour must have been considerable on these young men.

When I smilingly answered their challenge through my loud-hailer and invited two of them aboard they lost no time in coming alongside and boarding me. What was I to do then? Should we consider ourselves prisoners and behave with fitting humility or as hosts among friends and splice the main brace? I plumped for the latter and more pleasant course, and gave Heinz the order to offer them drinks, food or tea (a fitting national brew for such an occasion). But the boys were simply not having any. All our efforts at hospitality or conversation were cast aside, and we were bidden to keep station astern of the police launch.

At length we were within the Wismar pierheads. 'Go there,' ordered one of our boarding-party. We soon found ourselves made fast alongside the quay in the old harbour, opposite the frontier police station. Needless to say, a vast crowd collected at once. The people of Wismar were evidently impressed at the prospect of our imminent arrest.

Our two youths left us and were replaced by three other unsmiling and equally juvenile types, who proceeded to put us through a blistering interrogation. Meanwhile, the crowd alongside had swelled to immense proportions, doubtless in anticipation of the entertainment that this practical clash of ideologies might be expected to produce. I was thankful at this early stage to remember that I had been sent a letter of recommendation by the East German Yachting Association and this I produced.

It worked very well. The atmosphere quickly became less tense and it did not take us more than about two hours to get through the formalities. These were vastly complicated by the fact that every penny of money which each of us possessed had to be counted and entered on separate forms. This was done to prevent any 'black market' deals in the East German mark, which was officially quoted at parity with the West German D-Mark, but which was in fact worth only about a quarter of its official value.

The examination for spirits and tobacco, though thorough, was considerably more efficient and speedy than in Western Germany and certainly more polite than in England. We were given passes to go ashore, and the senior official, who remained behind after the others had gone, even unbent so far as to have a drink with us. By then, it seemed, our story about being bona-fide yachtsmen had been digested and believed. There may even have been a telephone call with Berlin.

Whenever I went on deck I smiled as pleasantly as possible at the gaping crowds and often invited them, especially the children, to come aboard and have a look around. This invitation was always met by a deprecatory gesture and the people I spoke to would then fade away. Meanwhile, our armed police guard paced resolutely up and down alongside us. By mingling with the crowd and talking to one or two of them, I was able to discover that in Eastern Germany no one—on pain of severe penalties—is allowed to board a foreign ship. Boarding a foreign vessel is the same as going abroad—a thing you must never do without permission.

That evening, as we were cooking dinner, two young men arrived with the news that they were a 'delegation' (in Communist countries almost everyone seems to be a delegation of some kind) from the local yacht club. We were delighted to see them (they had got permission from the police to come and see us) and after dinner I invited them and some of their friends to come aboard and have a drink. We passed a most pleasant evening; it was a demonstration of how people with the same interests in any country will tear down the barriers that their Governments may create.

I was a bit surprised to hear that capitalistic things like yacht clubs could exist in a Communist set-up. But they do: it works like this. The yachts are all owned by the club, which is known as a Betriebs Sport Gemeinschaft (Works Sports Union). The B.S.G. is a creation of the local shipyard or factory. It has many sections, each devoted to a particular sport. The yachting section is known as Sektion Segeln.

The shipyard is, in turn, of course, wholly owned by the State. Thus the yachts are all Government property. A member of the B.S.G. (Sektion Segeln) can obtain permission to use one of these commonly owned yachts from time to time by making application to the B.S.G. management, who decide whether his application is to be turned down or granted.

It is amazing that—in these dreary circumstances—there should be such keenness shown for yachting. Our Wismar hosts were keen to please and next day insisted on our having some small repairs done free of charge. They also brought me a copper plaque for my saloon—a gift which I found most touching.

We were allowed to wander at will and take photographs all over Wismar, which was once a fine Hanseatic town, but now gone sadly downhill. I changed some money at the official rate. This was a difficult job, as the one and only State bank was only open a few hours a day and I had to wander all over the place before finding a Customs man who would do it for me. I also watered, for the equivalent of 10s., a minimum rate which I found expensive.

The necessities of daily life which we had to buy in the rather uninspiring-looking shops were, we thought, reasonably priced, even at the artificial rate of the official exchange. Individuals that I spoke to were in every case polite and helpful. The only unpleasant atmosphere seemed to come from the officials themselves, who seemed to exercise a baneful influence on the population as a whole. It was, moreover, embarrassing to have an armed guard wandering up and down alongside us night and day.

By next morning the wind had moderated sufficiently for us to put to sea on our way to Warnemünde. My yachting friends warned me not to coast along, but to follow the buoyed channels until well outside the restricted areas, clearly marked on the chart. On no account must we go inside the restricted areas or make Rerik itself, even in stress of weather, for we should certainly be arrested. Rerik, they said, was full of Russians.

So we followed the buoyed channels and did what we were told. The Customs examination on sailing was fairly quickly over and we were glad to note the weather improving on passage. The longest of the legs that forenoon was made in sunshine and a slight following sea, giving us plenty of time to spruce ourselves up.

On reaching Warnemünde pierheads we were hailed and directed alongside a quay where a group of policemen and Customs officials were waiting. Before they had had a chance to come aboard, however, a pleasant young man jumped on to my quarter-deck and introduced himself to us as the secretary-general of the East German Yachting Association. We were altogether delighted to meet him, I especially so, in view of our friendly correspondence earlier that year, and we at once went below to open a bottle. It was, therefore, all the more disconcerting when a couple of policemen appeared aboard and dragged the secretary away with them.

To our great relief, he reappeared some time later and explained that what seemed like his arrest was due to his having transgressed the rule about not boarding foreign ships without permission. A telephone call to the right man in Berlin had, however, worked the usual miracle.

This is not the right place to dwell on the details of East German official hospitality. Suffice it to say that it was generous and—I think—sincere.

As in Wismar, the yachtsmen of Warnemünde were extremely kind. I was delighted to see the British flag flying at their club cross-trees, the first time since the war. We were taken on a sight-seeing tour to the adjacent city of Rostock, which the East Germans hope to make into a second Hamburg and there was an unexpected tour of the Warnow shipyards at Warnemünde, built since the war on reclaimed marshland and busily building 7,000- and 10,000-tonners, mostly for Soviet account. I don't know much about Soviet shipping, but the Soviet champagne we were offered was excellent and would, I think, be a great success in England if someone were to import it.

Our greatest pleasure as yachtsmen, however, was when we heard that two of our yachting friends from Warnemünde had been given permission to sail with us as far as the island of Hiddensee, our next port. Both these fellows were of the greatest help to us and we thoroughly enjoyed having them aboard. They were especially useful in making the approach to Kloster, the more northerly of Hiddensee's two ports. The channels around Hiddensee—and around the adjacent island of Rügen itself, were excellently marked, the Germans obviously having gone to great trouble to keep the channels marked and dredged. But it is absolutely essential to have the East German large-scale charts when navigating in this area, as they are the only ones which fully show the hazards.

We spent two nights alongside in Kloster harbour. The island people were very kind and a word from my escorting East Germans sufficed to keep the local police at arm's length. The island was charming and in great vogue as a holiday resort; it was a natural target for East German yachtsmen, of whom we met several.

The 3-hour trip from Kloster to Stralsund was made one Saturday forenoon in brilliant sunshine. The channel was splendidly marked and easily recognized, not only by the many buoys, but also by the surf breaking on the numerous banks. Approaching Stralsund harbour from the west, one has the choice of using the inner lead, which involves a lifting bridge, or the outer, which necessitates passing under a fixed railway bridge. We were met off the approaches by a launch from the Stralsund Yacht Club, which most kindly gave me an efficient pilot. This young man was one of the crew of an East German yacht which came to Cowes later that season, so I was especially glad to meet him. He advised against using the lifting bridge at the inner passage, as it lifted only at certain fixed times. We accordingly lowered our foremast and passed beneath the railway bridge. We then turned to starboard and soon found ourselves alongside in the yacht basin, where a number of vessels were preparing to sail on week-end cruises.

As elsewhere, the officials and members of the Stralsund Yacht Club did their utmost to make their unusual guests feel at home. The basin itself was not very good, especially when a wind blew, and we were covered in sand from the uncompleted quays. But I hear this trouble has now been remedied. It was, moreover, a long walk from the town and shops, but our berth at least had the supreme merit of quiet.

Changing money was another difficulty, as the Customs men were not accustomed to sterling and dollars and some curious situations developed, but the yacht club smoothed over these difficulties. We were three nights at Stralsund and thoroughly enjoyed ourselves. Entertainments included two visits to the theatre and a motor tour of the island of Rügen. We were also taken to a couple of restaurants (not bad food at all) and enjoyed excellent beer and aquavit.

On our sailing from Stralsund, the East Germans insisted on giving us a free fill of diesel fuel. They had also repaired our radio-telephone and one of the motor exhaust joints, all free of charge. I would have preferred to pay, but did not want to appear churlish. All we could do in return was to fill them all up with drinks.

Instead of proceeding out to sea, I had determined to take the inland waterways along the East German coastline to the Polish frontier. To give us a hand, the man who was later destined for Cowes was allowed to sail with us. He took the wheel all the way next day and I was very pleased to be able to relax and enjoy the passing scenery. On passage, we were in radio contact with Radio Rügen, which is the station which covers most of this area. The wind was westerly, Force 6, so we had it astern of us and made a very pleasant passage through the stretch of semi-enclosed water known as the Greifswalder Bodden. The channel was well marked, with a least depth of 18 ft.

The lighthouse on the islet of Ruden was the point for which we steered whilst crossing the Bodden, but about a mile before reaching it we altered course inshore at the Friensendorfer Haken Beacon and soon found ourselves entering the mouth of the River Peene. To port, the small town and harbour of Peenemünde came up. My pilot pointed out the buildings where the fuel for the V1 and V2 weapons had been made. Peenemünde seemed to be a fairly important naval base, for the hulls of many warships were plainly visible in its harbour.

It was not long before we reached Wolgast, a pleasant enough small town, undamaged by the war, where the shipbuilding yards were busy

14. East Germany to Poland

building small naval craft. Here our pilot disembarked, after kindly making arrangements for our clearing Customs next day. We spent the night alongside the quay and the skipper of a powerful postwar river tug showed us over his craft. We were not worried by police or other formalities in this port: in fact, the farther we got into Eastern Germany, the less our police and Customs troubles became. Possibly the Berlin authorities had put in a word for us.

We sailed at 1000 next day. It was still blowing, but fortunately still from the west, so that we had a following breeze all day. We at times had a little difficulty in finding our way, as the channel to begin with was not very clearly marked in some of the wider stretches. The charts indicated a least depth of about 6 ft, with many deeper parts. There was almost no traffic. Navigation at night would probably have been easier, for everywhere there were leading lights. At Zecherin bridge, connecting the island of Usedom with the mainland, we hoisted the signal indicated, any two flags one above the other, and the bridge lifted.

Normally, a vessel using these waterways passing from Eastern Germany into Poland should go into one of the two East German frontier ports of Uckermünde or Kaminke and clear, but our hosts had arranged for us not to have to make this detour. Instead, we were met by a frontier launch after passing the Karnin bridge (in construction) as we entered the large salt-lake called the Stettiner Haff across which the Polish–East German frontier runs.

We reduced speed and two youthful officials—Customs and police—boarded us. They were both friendly but efficient, so that the 'formalities' were over more quickly than I had expected. They showed no disposition to leave us—could it have been the whisky?—and after a while their skipper aboard the launch astern showed his displeasure by coming alongside and making things very clear through his loud-hailer. They left us reluctantly and we were once more on our own, heading out across the lake towards Poland. For the first time for twenty years, a British yacht wore the Polish flag at her cross-trees.

Our arrival in Poland was not exactly auspicious. We passed the line of black-and-white buoys marking the frontier across the Stettiner Haff without incident. The East Germans had told me I ought to clear Customs at a small port called Trzebiez (formerly Gross Ziegenort) situated at the point where the River Oder flows into the Haff. The place was so small that even the large-scale local charts scarcely showed it, but there was a remark on one of them 'entry marked by buoys' and this we resolved to take. So far, we had seen no shipping except the East German frontier control vessel stationed at anchor at the Repzin buoy just inside the frontier, but she had not challenged us.

As we made our way up the narrow approach channel to Trzebiez, our echo-sounder showed less and less water and it was no surprise to me when we finally found ourselves aground on sand, about a cable off the harbour mouth. By judiciously going astern we worked our way off without damage and crept cautiously into the harbour, where we found a large selection of East German barges. Their skippers told me that they had come down the Oder from Berlin and points inland and were waiting for the weather to improve before carrying on westward to the places we had just left. The only Polish official to greet us was a sleepy-looking soldier carrying a frightening-looking gun and smoking a cigarette. He did not seem very interested in us and it was some while before I could persuade him to go to find an officer and get the formalities started. He came back after about half an hour with an officer who told us that clearance could not be effected here: we were to continue upriver to Szczecin (formerly Stettin), where everything would happen.

Our entry into Poland was thus a far less efficient and frightening affair than into East Germany. We were later to find, in fact, that things in Poland were very different from those in East Germany in all respects. The standard of living, to begin with, seemed much lower. The efficiency was much less. On the other hand, there was a very much greater measure of freedom, especially freedom of speech. To our amazement, everyone seemed to speak with absolute freedom about their Government, the state of the country and, in fact, all matters. In Eastern Germany, such a thing could never happen—the Communist control was far too strict. Poland, however, seemed only theoretically Communist. Before all else, the people were Poles and Westwards-looking. Added to this, one could reckon with a great natural politeness and charm of manner, even in the uneducated classes, so that an immediate sympathy for these unfortunate people was created.

It was a lovely summer evening trip up the calm broad Oder to

Szczecin. The small amount of traffic that we passed included a large
Polish yacht called the *Joseph Conrad*, whose crew—seeing our unusual flag
—called out cheerfully to us to join them. As we approached Szczecin, we
saw notices in Polish and English on the river banks stating that 'The
Oder-Neisse line is a line of peace'. Poor old peace again! The Admiralty

15. The new Polish coastline

chart of the river and approaches to Szczecin was used throughout and
was found to be complete and accurate.

Aided by the chart, we made fast to a quay on our starboard hand on
arrival. It was opposite the building that housed the Polish State pilotage
service for bringing merchantmen up and down the River Oder between
Szczecin and Swinoujscje (formerly Swinemuende). We were greeted by a
benevolent Customs official who immediately made us welcome to his
country. He did not seem particularly interested in what we had aboard,
but went off, saying he would be back shortly. This proved only too true,
for he brought with him a policeman, two port officials, another Customs
man and a ship chandler. I thought at first we were in for a difficult time
officially, but all they did was to urge me to take as much spirits as possible
from our bonded store, with which the entire gang proceeded to make
merry until the early hours. It was all very muddled and charming and at
the end of it I was not at all sure who had cleared whom or what.

Next day we were invited to lunch ashore by some delightful Poles to whom I had been given an introduction. We were also interviewed by the Polish Radio. One of the questions put to me was: 'How have our officials behaved towards you?' Two fellows representing the local yacht club (in Poland they are organized in the same way as in Eastern Germany) came aboard and kindly invited us to sail as soon as possible for Swinoujscje, where a regatta was being held and where we were apparently expected.

Next morning at 1100 we cast off from Szczecin without formalities and proceeded downriver to the Haff, which we entered some two hours later. At this point I called up Radio Szczecin and asked them to warn Swinoujscje of our imminent arrival. The operator spoke good English. We passed through the curious artificial canal which gives direct access from the Haff to Swinoujscje and as we were getting close to it a launch came towards us bearing several important-looking people in yachting caps. Fortunately, we were looking reasonably smart ourselves, having just washed down and spruced ourselves up, so that when two Polish yachtsmen came aboard we did not have to feel ashamed of ourselves. The two visitors turned out to be the secretary-general of the Polish Yachting Association, who happened to be in Swinoujscje for the regatta, and the president of the regatta committee. The Association secretary had been in England quite a lot and spoke English, and the president spoke good German, so we were able to express our mutual pleasure at meeting fairly fluently. Both of them were most welcoming and—like all Poles—delightful to talk to. We enjoyed a cup of tea together on the quarter-deck as we neared the port.

Swinoujscje was quite an important port, as it is at the entry to the Szczecin approaches and every merchantman bound for Szczecin has to pass it, though most of them do no more than take on or drop a pilot. It was also the most important Soviet naval base in Poland, full of Russian warships and seamen. We saw some of these, as well as Polish warships, as we continued down the canal, and for the first time in my life I found myself dipping to the Hammer and Sickle. They answered meticulously, staring at us as well they might, with some considerable interest.

A vast throng of people had gathered on the quay at Swinoujscje, where we were to make fast. Most of them were locals, but there was also a fair sprinkling of seamen and yachtsmen attending the local regatta, which we were told was the first that had been held at Swinoujscje since the war. For the town had only recently been 'handed back' by the Soviet Navy for use by Polish civilians. Most of it looked very dilapidated. *September Tide* lay stern on to a jetty with one anchor out forward. The holding-ground later proved not very good, but it seemed all right at the time, as there was almost no wind.

Some policemen and Customs officials came aboard and rather half-heartedly started to go through their usual drill. One of them was quite a pretty girl, who afterwards came to see us *en civil*. There was also an attempt to station an armed police guard at our gangway, but this was abandoned after some representations by the yacht club. We were then taken ashore to dine. It was all very jolly.

We spent in all five days in Swinoujscje, all of them fascinating. Two regatta courses were being sailed. The longer, naturally only for the larger boats, was across to the 'Falsterbo Rev' lightship at the southern point of Sweden, around the Danish island of Bornholm and thence homewards. This was expected to take some four or five days to accomplish, depending on the winds. The shorter course, for smaller yachts, was only about 12 miles along the coast to the little resort of Miedzyzdroje (formerly Misdroy) and back again. The yachtsmen were unanimous in their condemnation of the police, who kept a very strict control over all that went on. Yachts were searched before sailing and on returning and were not allowed to deviate from the prescribed course. Sometimes there seemed to be almost as many police on the quayside as yachtsmen. I inquired the reason for this and was told that recently some Polish yachtsmen had 'escaped' from their country to the neighbouring Danish island of Bornholm—apparently a favourite haven for escaping Easterners generally—and since then police precautions had been greatly increased. It seemed that a larger yacht, with permission to sail from Swinoujscje to Gdynia, had, in fact, done a bunk direct to Bornholm with all aboard. Several canoe-loads of Poles had done the same thing from various points along the coast.

Yachtsmen in Poland fell into three categories: those who wished only to use inland waters, who needed to provide themselves with no official documents; those who wished to sail offshore, who must get a so-called 'sea-card' written in Polish and English, which gave them the right to sail at sea, but not to land foreign; and finally those very favoured few who, generally after months of effort, found themselves furnished with an *ad hoc* passport (withdrawn on return) which made it possible not only to leave Poland legally, but also to land on foreign soil. With that concession, however, the Polish Government doubtless felt satisfied, since each man was only given three U.S. dollars with which to sustain existence during the whole of his foreign cruise.

'Why don't more of you from England come to see us?' the skipper of the *Joseph Conrad* asked me when I went to dine aboard with him. The Poles are most Westward-looking and it is a great pity that one, in fact, sees so little of them. For a Polish yacht to gain permission to come to British waters, she must first be 'invited' by some British yacht club, otherwise the Polish Government would not issue the necessary exit permits. This sounded quite incredible to us, but unfortunately to the Polish yachting fraternity it was a grim and inevitable reality. All the yachtsmen I met begged me to make it clear to British yacht clubs that these 'invitations' were a mere formality which, on being asked, they could issue without the slightest fear of being landed with a bunch of assorted Polish yachtsmen for the rest of their lives. With Europe in her present state, it seems such a small thing for a club to be willing to do and I hope that all who may read this will take heed and thus encourage goodwill among yachtsmen, regardless of political creeds.

There were several East German yachts in Swinoujscje for the regatta, some from Warnemünde, and we were able to send our good wishes back to East German yachtsmen by this means. As we had no police guard, we were able to invite Poles aboard at will, and it was a great pleasure to be able to repay some of their hospitality in this way. There were solemn warnings about thieves and each night we used to stow all movable gear below. In this way we limited our losses to a pair of rowlocks—not bad for nearly a week's stay.

I tried one day to sail our dinghy down to the harbour mouth and around to the beach for a swim, but was turned back just in time. Not only was it apparently necessary for me to clear Customs for such an operation, but the Soviet warships stationed at the harbour mouth would have taken a very dim view of this. So we were confined to sailing the dinghy up and down the basin. The crews of the Soviet warships used to indulge in this sport, too, presumably out of sheer boredom. The Poles, who didn't seem at all friendly towards their Russian allies, refused to speak to them and the Russians themselves seemed to have non-fraternizing orders. On the other hand, one or two individual Russians of both sexes whom I met wandering around the town seemed polite and friendly while alone with me. What a strange world!

It ultimately became necessary for us to return to Szczecin upriver for one of my crew to board a U.K.-bound ship. Among the Poles, there was some consternation at this news, and the delightful committee president came aboard to explain that this would involve a police search of our vessel. In order that we would not suffer the humiliation of this search in public, we were asked to cross the river and undergo it on the other side. It seemed tactful to agree to this, but when we at last got over the other side, the police told us it was not necessary, so we sailed forthwith on the 4-hour trip back to Szczecin, where we berthed in the same place as before.

I was intending to sail that same night, but I received a most kind invitation to the Regatta Ball that evening, so decided to delay departure until next morning. This was the first function of its kind that I had been to in a Communist country and so I found it very interesting, as much for the variety of costume worn as for any other reason. As I expected, the Polish ladies were enchanting. After the prize-giving, the leader of the East German delegation made a lengthy speech and presented the astonished Poles with a photograph of a ferry-boat which I was told had recently been completed for the German–Swedish run.

Feeling somewhat the worse for wear, I was preparing to cast off next morning, when I remembered that we had been told to ask for police and Customs clearance before sailing. So I hurriedly rang up and asked. It was, however, over 2 hours before the men turned up and I recalled too late that I had been warned that in Poland you always had to ask for clearance at least 2 hours before you needed it. I expect this was to give them time to check up on you before arriving.

When they at last turned up complications seemed legion and we were thoroughly fed up with the lot of them. I began to regret my complimentary remarks over the Polish Radio about their officials! To begin with, the Immigration men said that my visa issued by the Polish Embassy in London was valid for one entry only and that I must now leave the country. This produced a tremendous argument, but at last they seemed willing to take the view that, as we had never spent a night ashore and had thus never technically entered Poland at all, we would be permitted to go on our way.

One of the officers then summoned four soldiers, who proceeded to search the ship from stem to stern. Glad as I was of this chance of showing them around my property, I was a little mystified as to what it was all about until I was given the hint that it was to prevent Polish yachtsmen stowing away with us. I had warned them that we did not intend to clear at Swinoujscje, but to proceed from Szczecin downriver and then straight out to sea to the eastward, so they were, I suppose, determined to see that no stowaways came with us from the start. This seemed reasonable, bearing in mind where one was.

But when we at last cast off a powerful police launch lying close by cast off, too, and followed us a cable or less astern all the way downriver. We anchored at the entrance to the Haff to wash down our sides and the launch was made fast at an adjacent pier. When we weighed, she again took up station astern of us and did not leave us until we were well outside Swinoujscje pierheads. Whilst fully admitting the rights of the Poles to do what they like to visitors in Poland, it seemed to us hard on Polish yachtsmen that they were apparently considered so anxious to leave their fatherland that extreme measures of this kind had to be taken. Perhaps if more British yachts were to go there, things might become a bit easier. After all, we reflected, we were only the thin end of a possible wedge.

The coastal trip from Swinoujscje pierheads—where we dipped to a flotilla of Polish destroyers entering harbour—to Kolobrzeg (formerly Kolberg), a distance of 50 miles, was accomplished against the weather and took us 7 hours. We sighted no shipping and the only seamark encountered was the landfall buoy off the small port of Dievenow. The coast was low and sandy, but with sufficient landmarks to make out clearly where we were. We made the rather tricky entry at Kolobrzeg before sunset.

September Tide was grateful to Kolobrzeg for its quiet welcome. Tired out by our long day and the departure from Szczecin, we were eagerly looking forward to turning in. It was therefore with more than usual gratitude that we received a kindly Polish policeman aboard and heard him tell us that, our papers being in order, he would leave us to our slumbers at once.

Nevertheless, a guard was posted at the gangway. We slept well, although during the night I recall telling the guard that we would appreciate it if the spectators would talk less loudly. Silence at once fell and we slept the sleep of the just.

I was most embarrassed next morning when a Customs man arrived, hot and tired, and told me he had come all the way from Ustka—our next port of call—by cross-country train specially to see us. It seemed there was no Customs post at Kolobrzeg and so he had been sent over to clear us, a matter of five minutes' work. We felt most apologetic at causing all this trouble.

The representative of the local branch of Baltona, the Polish State ship chandlers, came aboard and, speaking good English and German, kindly offered to show us around. I gladly accepted his invitation, as a result of which we had a comprehensive tour of the ruined city, ending up with a visit to quite a good restaurant, with music and dancing, which had apparently risen Phoenix-like from the ruins. The food was good. We drank beer. I noticed a bottle of Côtes du Rhône which we had been used to buying in France for about 10s. priced at over £10.

Baltona is an excellent institution if you have foreign exchange to offer. They supplied us with the necessities of daily life in almost every port. I always paid in dollars or sterling but, even at the official tourist rate of exchange of 67 zloty to the £, prices were quite reasonable. Officially, there were only about 10 zloty to a £, and on the black market, which we never dared to patronize, I was told you could get up to 300. We had bought some zloty officially at the bank in Szczecin and these few notes made it possible for us to buy things like bread, fruit and vegetables, which were not worth getting at the ship chandlers. Meat could also be bought, but it involved a lot of queueing and was not always available, so we rather gave up bothering about it. Prices for the things we did need were on the whole quite fair, but of course we never shopped for anything except the bare necessities.

We said good-bye to Kolobrzeg with some regret—they had been very kind to us—and spent 8 hours of June 28 sailing along the Polish coast towards Ustka (formerly Stolpmuende), which we had planned as our next port of call. Navigation was extremely easy, with good visibility and almost a flat calm. We set course at first for Jaroslavice lighthouse some 42 sea-miles distant, thus losing sight of land for some while. Thereafter the familiar pattern of the Polish coastline again came into view—the sand-dunes, the low-lying dark forests and the evenly spaced watch-towers, grim reminders of the totalitarian State. There was no traffic and the only worth while township passed was the little port of Darlowo.

We entered Ustka pierheads at 1715. Encouraged by our happy experiences at Kolobrzeg, we were greatly looking forward to visiting yet another small Polish harbour. The gay flags and bunting that decorated the ships and buildings as we approached (in celebration of the Polish Week of the Sea) made us feel all the happier, and the crowds of sightseers lining the quays added yet another festive note to the scene.

No sooner were we fast than our troubles began. Some worried officials came aboard and told us that we could not land. A cordon was thrown around the quay and the crowd were kept away from us. I started to photograph the quayside scene, but a policeman came up and told me to put my camera away. Feeling embarrassed and rather unwanted, we remained below. Later, however, I came up on deck and a woman in the crowd shouted out in German: 'Cheer up! One of these days we'll get together—despite them!' The crowd took up her cry and I waited with some anxiety for her to be arrested, but to my relief nothing happened. Maybe the police secretly sympathized. I would have moved to the next port rather than stay where we were not wanted, but we were feeling very tired. I was alone with Heinz, my faithful German hand, and the boat was about as big as two men could manage, so we did not want to overdo it.

It was 2½ hours before the officials returned and almost too dark for me to take the photographs to which I had been looking forward. They seemed in better form this time and were accompanied by an extremely nice man who, in addition to his duties as Ustka harbour master, was also Commodore of the local yacht club. We were given passes to go ashore and the Commodore lost no time in inviting us to join him on a sightseeing tour. At the police cordon we had to show our passes, both coming and going, and nobody was allowed near us. The Commodore was one of nature's gentlemen: he showed us all over his town, gave us a glass of beer in the seamen's home and invited us to look over an 'artists' holiday home' where, by some process known only to Maskelyne and Cook, forty people were lodged at a time. After dark, we gave him dinner aboard and admired a firework display given by the Polish Navy.

Next morning as we were leaving the Commodore appeared in full harbour master's gold braid and presented me with a burgee of his yacht club. I was most touched and returned the gesture with one of mine.

The eleven-hour run from Ustka to Hela was easily accomplished, again in calm. Landmarks, other than lighthouses, which stood out from the monotonous sand-dunes like candles on a birthday cake, were few. Over to starboard after a couple of hours' going we could see the little port of Leba, with its notorious sandbar. After lunch, the headland of Rozewie with its important lighthouse loomed close; the fishing-harbour of Wladislawowo; the long low peninsula of Hela; some wrecks rusting close inshore; some sort of military installation near the beach and suddenly we rounded the point. The Bay of Danzig opened out before us and close by were the pier-heads of Hela.

In contrast to those at Ustka, the Hela officials were most friendly and helpful and the formalities were over in less than five minutes. We dined ashore so badly at a restaurant called the 'Riviera' that it was funny, and the locals, sensing our amusement, joined in the laughter, and a good time was had by all. Sightseeing in such a small place was limited to a few Dutch-style houses said to have been built by a shipload of shipwrecked Dutch seamen who had settled there when Hela was an island.

Refreshed by a good night's sleep, we cleared quickly and sailed on the short leg to Gdynia across the bay. From the chart, the westernmost entry seemed the most convenient. We were nearing it with official letters flying when a shot rang out from the pierheads. Sensing trouble, I naturally stopped. A group of seamen, waving frantically towards the east, appeared on the look-out tower and I altered course for the next entrance. Here, however, another frenzied group appeared, again waving us eastward, so that I had no alternative but to steam eastward until we reached the last entrance, whence access to the yacht basin—marked on the Admiralty chart—was clear. We made fast alongside the Fishery School, were asked to move to another berth and finally ended up stern to the quay opposite the Stal Yacht Club, one of the five that line the basin. Three extremely pleasant Poles, representing the local yachting fraternity, came aboard and we at once felt at home. Police supervision here was limited to a constant

patrol up and down the quayside; no one was actually posted at our gangway. At night occasional green flares lit the sky above the basin; the ever-
vigilant police were on the lookout to prevent Poles escaping.

Gdynia was a nice place. There was more life about the town than we
had noted to date and we were able to make excursions by train to Sopot,
Oliva and Danzig, all very rewarding. Baltona, the chandlery, were most
helpful, although to our consternation our cooking-gas cylinders were not
rechargeable there and the Polish gas cylinders were much too big to ship
in any yacht. The Stal Yacht Club, sponsored by the local shipyard, was
most kind and took the trouble to entertain us at the clubhouse one evening,
when I was happy to make an interchange of burgees. Fresh water was laid
on to the quay; a British courtesy flag was flown and we were honoured
with a visit from several distinguished Poles.

To my great delight, a visit to a regatta which was being sailed on the
Zalew Vislany (formerly Frisches Haff) was proposed. I knew that we
would be visiting waters which no Western eyes had seen since the war.
Three Polish yachtsmen had miraculously secured permission to sail with
me. We filled in papers in triplicate and then we were off.

Past the famous pier at Sopot, past the busy harbour approaches of
Danzig and soon we entered the mouth of the Dead Vistula at a little place
known as Gorki Wslodwie, where we passed through a police control. The
Vistula in its lower reaches splits into several distinct streams. It has three
mouths, of which we had taken the central.

As soon as we were inside the Vistula we saw a multitude of sailing
yachts and several clubs, some of which made us welcome signals, to which
we gladly replied. My Polish yachting guests were most useful and I was
able to let them take the wheel almost all the time, while I relaxed and
enjoyed the delights of the Polish scene. At Prezegalina we locked into the
Vistula proper, taking in tow a small Polish sailing yacht which was also
regatta-bound. Our masts just passed beneath the road bridge at the lock,
which was not due to swing open until some hours later. In the Vistula
main stream, the current was estimated at about $1\frac{1}{2}$ knots.

After less than an hour in the main river, we turned to port into the
Gdanska locks and passed into the section of the Vistula known as the
Elbing Vistula, which was to lead us all the way into the Frisches Haff. My
echo-sounder throughout registered about 12 ft of water beneath our keel.

At 1700 we entered the wide, shallow, brackish lake known to the Poles as the Zalew Vislany. Up to the end of the war the Germans maintained a channel through it from Elblag (formerly Elbing) to join the sea at Pillau, so that ships built in the inland waterways could pass through, but now that the somewhat artificial Russian–Polish frontier prevented egress to Polish shipping at the Russian-held port of Pillau (now known as Baltyisk), it was not worth while for the Poles to keep it dredged. The whole of the Haff, therefore, had a maximum depth of some 10 ft.

It seemed, too, that the buoyage system had recently been changed, so that both the Admiralty and the Polish charts we carried were wrong. Nevertheless, we arrived safely off Krinica Morska (formerly Kahlberg), where the regatta was being held, and the Poles, in their usual disarmingly charming way, sent out a yacht to lead us in flying a signal of welcome.

We enjoyed ourselves more in Krinica Morska than anywhere else in Poland. This was doubtless due to the absence of police and Customs to worry us, the pleasure we felt at some Polish yachtsmen aboard with us, and the sincere and wonderful hospitality we enjoyed. This included an impromptu picnic on the grass with the crews of some other boats, followed by a visit to the local pub and an evening enlivened by the joys of whisky and vodka. One really felt one was getting somewhere. Speeches were made to welcome us and I was able to reply—through an interpreter—sincerely stressing our joy at being there. I think at this stage the Poles were really beginning to believe that I had come to Poland as a private citizen, that my visit was not paid for or backed by any Government or other organization and that the yacht belonged to me.

Next morning (I admit to feeling somewhat the worse for wear) my naval chum from Gdynia turned up in a fast Polish Navy motor launch and invited us to join him and his party in a trip across the Haff to Frombork (Frauenburg). We gladly accepted and made a fast crossing to view the historic town with its red brick cathedral and house where the medieval astronomer Copernicus made his discoveries.

On returning to Krinica Morska, we set out for Elblag (formerly Elbing) the industrial town up the canal on the other side of the Haff. Some yachtsmen had missed the regular connection and we were able to give them a lift. It was a wonderful sensation to be able to do a kindness of this sort without having to ask permission in writing in triplicate or getting into trouble for having done it. Evidently, once one was inside Poland, as distinct from merely being on the sea-board, things became much easier and I began to regret not accepting the hinted invitation to continue to Warsaw.

The canal up to Elblag was a delightful trip in the sunset, but the fine old town was terribly damaged. The shipyards were dead, but several boat and yacht clubs miraculously lingered on the canal banks. One of them, doubtless sponsored by the electricity works, was called the 'Energetic'.

A night in Elblag, where we admired the curious narrow launches which are hauled overland in the area of the Masurian Lakes. This would also make an interesting motor-boat excursion. A passage back along the canal and again we found ourselves out in the Haff. We had a rendezvous there with some of the yachts from the regatta, but they were not to be seen, so we went on our way into the Elbing Vistula again. Some Russian patrol boats could be seen exercising on the Haff. At the railway bridge in the river we were again forced to stop. The Russians seemed dangerously close astern and soon to my dismay they were coming alongside us.

I imagined we were again in for one of those unpleasant periods of explaining, but to everyone's surprise they appeared quite friendly. We actually made fast to each other and I was about to take some photographs when the bridge opened and the two patrol boats were off like a bomb.

We caught up with them later in the Gdanska Glowa and Przegalina locks and, although conversation was quite hopeless, I managed to persuade one of the skippers to come aboard and presented him with twenty Players, with whose seamanlike appearance he seemed greatly impressed.

It was glorious weather and the last lap of the trip across the Bay of Danzig was a fitting conclusion to my yachting in Polish waters. Next morning, however, our troubles were to start again. I wanted to sail and first to fuel. This does not sound difficult, but in Gdynia it was not all that easy. After a lot of talk with the ship chandlers, we obtained police permission to shift berth into the commercial harbour, where we waited for some time before the right man arrived to open the pumps. This at last effected, we had to go back to the yacht basin and report to the police that we wished to leave. They took an age coming and our Polish yachting friends, who had meanwhile collected in force to bid us farewell, began tactfully to melt away so as not to witness the final humiliation of our vessel being searched—not for contraband, but for stowaway Poles.

The officers conducting this ritual, when they at length appeared, were not unduly tiresome and I was able to offer them refreshment as my last act in Poland without feeling too irritated.

At last we were allowed to leave and I set course out across the Bay and thence past all the old familiar landmarks. On rounding Hela into the open sea I made a couple of R/T signals thanking the Poles for all they had done, and Gdynia Radio gave me a forecast of wind nor'-west 2–4 for the night.

On rounding Rozewie Point we got the wind right in our teeth, there was some water shipped and for a moment I considered putting back into Wladislawowo. But valour prevailed over prudence and, on a steady course 278, we continued into it. Bornholm lay out there, somewhere over the horizon.

5
Scandinavian Interlude

Denmark, Norway and Sweden
each provides its individual delights

After the rigours of Communism, it was a sheer delight to find oneself in the tiny but well-ordered harbour of Gudhjem in Bornholm. After satisfying the cravings of the local Press as to how we had 'escaped from Poland', I set course north for the diminutive pair of rocks in the Baltic known as Christiansoe. The island's governor was an old friend of mine and we had quite a reunion over a bottle of Danish 'Akvavit' that evening. The island's atmosphere rather resembled that of the French island of Chausey, the only one in the English Channel; needless to say, it was a regular yachtsman's port of call.

From Christiansoe, we sailed westwards to the Swedish port of Ystad and thence to Nyhavn Canal in the very centre of Copenhagen. Our fame seemed to have preceded us, for we were immediately a magnet for the Danish Press, and I had the distinction of my portrait being plastered over the town as an intrepid explorer who had only just managed to return from the Communist jaws of death. I hoped that if ever my Polish and East German hosts read these lurid accounts, they would not be taking Western journalism too literally.

It is always difficult for a yacht to make up her mind where to lie in the delightful city of Copenhagen. The Nyhavn Canal has the great advantage of being in the centre of the city, but it is naturally far from clean and the somewhat uncontrolled night-life that flourishes around it is rather unsettling. Besides, if there is a wind, the refuse from the streets blows all over one's decks and one has to go around sweeping up bits of straw and horse-manure all day. After a few days of this, I sailed for the headquarters of the Royal Danish Yacht Club at a place about six miles north of the town called Skovshoved. We had also gone to look at the Yacht Basin at Lange Linie, near where the Little Mermaid keeps her lonely vigil, but decided that, of the places we could use, Skovshoved was much the best.

Nor were we disappointed. Apart from providing all facilities such as fresh water, fuel, and a safe berth, the staff of the club could not do too much for us, and we spent a most agreeable week there. It was true that the club was some way from the centre of the town, but in summer a lot of the city's life moves out to the Sound and we had many friends in the locality on whose hospitality we sponged unashamedly.

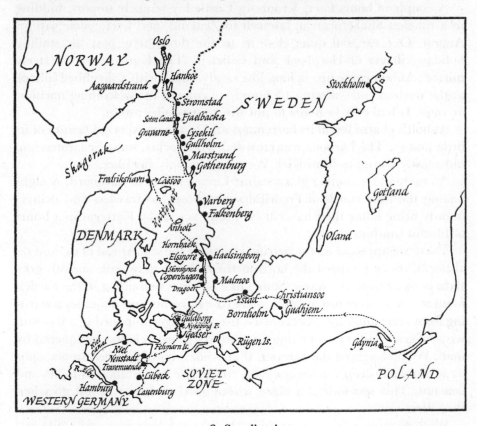

16. Scandinavia

It was time to move on to fresh fields. I had already once enjoyed a superb cruise in Swedish waters up the Eastern Swedish skerries to Stockholm and thence across Sweden through the sixty-three locks of the Goeta Canal down to Gothenburg. It seemed appropriate now to attempt the passage up the Swedish West Coast Skerries to Oslo.

And so we slipped from the hospitable berth off the Royal Danish Yacht Club at Skovshoved and made for the Danish island of Anholt, midway up the Kattegat. I had decided not to go direct up the lower part of the Swedish coast; some years ago I had visited such ports as Falkenberg and Varberg. The facilities there were good, but the scenery was unrewarding, not worthy of being revisited.

A couple of hours later, Kronborg Castle lay serenely to port, bidding us a timeless Shakespearean farewell to Zealand, and I set course 316 for Anholt. One can sail quite close in to the shore here, past the smiling holiday villages of Hornbaek and Gilleleje. The Kattegat was a steely mirror; Anholt came up—a long low sandy island with a shrubbed hillock at the western end—around 1800 and we entered the welcoming harbour at 1930. It had cost 11 hours to put the 77 sea-miles astern.

Anholt's charm lies in its barrenness and in the unexpected beauty of its little houses. The harbour was crowded with yachts, some Scandinavian, but mostly Germans from Kiel. We were the only Britisher.

An early start; another glassy calm; Laesoe Island to starboard. A night among the fishy smells of Fredrikshavn, whose 300 trawlers and drifters nightly bring home their harvest. Next day across the Kattegat in 4 hours of blissful sunshine.

There we approached the petrified forest of the sea. Ahead of us, and on either beam as I ranged the horizon through the glass, rose smooth grey slabs of stone from the water. Some, like tortoises swimming in the garden pond at home, were just awash; others rose towering and majestic, a warning from afar; and others beckoned a friendly finger, supporting a few thin wisps of grass and even sometimes a small red wooden house, conquered by man. We had sighted the Skerries, that wilderness of polished stones, split by a thousand deep waterways, each made safe by numberless lights and beacons. This was indeed a place where good yachtsmen must go when they die.

We passed the curious triangular obelisk on Vinga islet and made our approach to Gothenburg accordingly. I had called Gothenburg Radio and given our E.T.A. as 1630, so it was a matter of prestige to arrive on time off the private harbour of the Royal Swedish Yacht Club. At Vinga we knew that the Skerries had really begun. Anxious at first at the new sensation of being encased in rocks and feeling like a beginner in the Hampton Court Maze, we slackened speed. But the echo-sounder showed great depths, even quite close to the dangers. Navigation with the excellent Swedish large-scale charts was easy and all the marks came up exactly where expected.

The yacht harbour at Gothenburg was some miles out of the main town at a place aptly named Lange Drag. It was a tiresome and expensive business getting into town by taxi, but the berth was spotlessly clean and the boatman and ship chandler most attentive. The Customs—though less efficient and more aggressive than in Denmark, were courteous. I was thankful, at the end of the ordeal, to be given a list of our stores to show at other Swedish ports—a great time-saver for all.

Marstrand has long been the goal of international—including many British—yachtsmen and that was to be our next port of call. There are several routes northward from Gothenburg to this enchanting place, but we decided to take that most used by the local steamer traffic. Despite the grey day, the journey was a delight. Some Swedish friends had embarked to give me a hand with the navigation, but this proved quite unnecessary, the channels being all so extremely well marked. In particular the last lap of the afternoon's trip was shockingly beautiful as we passed through the narrow Albrechtsund leading into the Marstrand approaches, almost touching the houses on either side.

We berthed stern to the quay at Marstrand, where there were quite a number of yachts. Fortunately for us, the current was not running very strongly, so that we had time to drop an anchor before being swept away sideways, and quickly placed our stern to. If one were allowed a criticism of this disturbingly lovely place, I would say that it is quite extraordinary that the Swedes do not lay on proper fresh-water facilities in a spot where there are so many potential customers.

But maybe one should not look a gift horse in the mouth. The little island, made famous as a tourist resort by King Oskar II, who often visited it, consists of a picturesque meandering village alongside the quay, a rather

too-expensive and too-noisy grand hotel, a fine medieval fortress crowning
the whole, and a profusion of smooth assorted boulders sloping down to
coves that cry aloud for bathers to plunge into them. The Swedes all seemed
fascinated by a tram-like electric ferry that connected the island with the
mainland a cable or so away. There was a curious Mary-Rose quality
about the island that even the day-tourists did nothing to dispel. At midnight I climbed alone to the fortress to look out over the long tired broken
coastline, watched over by the countless blinking lighthouses, and knew I
had come to an unusual place.

It is one of the few disadvantages of yachting in Swedish waters that one
cannot call up on the R/T and get a weather forecast, at least not without
paying a fabulous sum. Nor do the Swedish coastal radio stations emit any
regular weather bulletins. So that, if the B.B.C. is out of range, one has to
guess what is coming. Opposed to this, however, is the overwhelming
advantage that it doesn't, after all, very much matter what the weather
does in these sheltered waters, which, with their myriad islands, can always
afford a lee close at hand.

Two nights in Marstrand and we were ready for sea again. I had heard
much of Lysekil as the place to which our fast launches sped on moonless
nights during the war to fetch ball-bearings from the Swedes. I had also
heard that Sonja Henje was summering there. Anyway, it was our goal for
the next day. There were several alternative routes, but the most interesting seemed to be the inner passage up the broad approaches to Uddevalla,
thence to port and finally through a web of rocks and islets and debouching
suddenly into the Lysekil approaches themselves.

The scenery on passage was utterly satisfying. Smooth grey rocks, pine
trees and small red wooden houses seemed to be the keynote. Some two
hours out of Marstrand, we came to a tangle of bridges spanning the fjord
at an island called Kaelloe. One bridge was in process of erection by a
German firm, whose guard-boat waved us away to another gap. It seemed
a miracle that in this remote place so gossamer a structure was being flung
across the fjord.

My log notes that this was our worst day to date. Re-reading it, I was
struck by such a statement. But, reading further, I saw what inspired it. In
the last 2 hours before reaching Lysekil, we found ourselves caught up in
the passage of the tortuous narrows north of Flatoen Island which provide

25. Gudhjim harbour on Bornholm Island is the most popular with yachtsmen on this island.

26. This narrow metal bridge links the two islands that form Christiansoe, the smallest and most remote island in the Kingdom of Denmark.

27. Marstrand. A view from the fortress towards the mainland.

28. Gullholm. General view.

29. Looking across the Sound from Gravarne to Smoegen.

30. A view of Gravarne, the charming skerries fishing port which gives a warm welcome to yachtsmen.

31. The Lysekil yacht basin with the author's yacht *September Tide* stern to the quay.

32. Dronningen, the Oslo clubhouse of the Royal Norwegian Y.C. with *September Tide* (left) and *Martinetta* (right).

a short cut across to Lysekil. On the chart, these looked easy enough to negotiate. But I had reckoned without the strong north-going currents that we were to encounter. These twice caught our ship and nearly put us on the rocks, had we not gone hard astern both engines. It is one thing to navigate an unknown difficult channel in peace and quiet with time to think, but when in the grip of a current one is forced sometimes to take decisions too quickly to be correct. Moreover, the channel was so narrow here that not even a large-scale chart could accurately show the buoyage. Had it not been for the help of a group of Swedes who, seeing our plight, ran alongside on the shore shouting directions, I doubt if we would have made it. At Lysekil, we had the choice of entering the small commercial harbour within the town or using the yacht basin. I chose the latter, which, despite being some distance from the town, seemed clean and quiet and full of promise of a good night's sleep.

After the tribulations of yesterday, it seemed desirable to take it easy. We were especially recommended to visit either Smoegen or Gravarne, two twin fishing villages about 11 miles to the north. On passage, I made the foolish mistake of doubting the Swedish chart, so that I found myself leaving a port-hand buoy to starboard in a narrow passage, with almost disastrous results. The echo-sounder gave a nil reading and, white with fear and remorse, we went on our way.

Arrived off Smoegen, we edged our way into the tiny rift in the rocks which forms the harbour, but it was obvious that there was no room for us. So we moved across the sound to Gravarne, about a mile away. Here we had a warm welcome from the hundreds of tourists that thronged the place. The harbour, with a fair quota of fishing-craft, was nevertheless big enough to take quite a few visitors.

The next day's leg was to be our last in Swedish waters. We planned to cover the 41 miles to Stroemstad, the last Swedish port and a well-known tourist resort which we had always been anxious to see.

Very soon after leaving Gravarne, we entered the Soten Canal, through which one is not allowed to proceed at a speed exceeding 5 knots. There is one bridge spanning the canal and it opens if the signal —— —— — is sounded on coming from southward. From the northward the signal —— —— — — must be made. There are no tolls. There is a least depth of about 16 ft in the canal, which is used by the medium-sized tourist ships which ply in summer between Oslo and Gothenburg.

It was another glorious summer's day and all along the leads there were Swedish yachts of all kinds to be seen. There was also the occasional Dane or Norwegian and we once saw a German, but no British. The highlights were the passage of a deep and narrow cleft at Hoernoe Ranne (where I saw the Royal Swedish Yacht Club had established a small clubhouse) and the delightful passage of the Hamburg sound, across which sprawls the doll's-house village of Hamburgsund. There is a least depth of about 15 ft in the channel.

Off the small resort of Fjaellbacka we noted the flat grey islet of Dannholm and I went as close as good manners allowed to get a photograph of Ingrid Bergman's house there. She owns the islet and the Swedish flag flying at her flagstaff doubtless showed that the star was at home. Close north of Dannholm we approached the beacon known as Djupskaer on which a lighthouse had so recently been established that it was not even shown on our chart.

One more narrow passage, the mile-long Havstensund, and we found ourselves in a broad fjord leading up to Stroemstad and the Norwegian frontier. By contrast with the other places we had called at since leaving Gothenburg, Stroemstad gave a big-city impression. It boasted several hotels, restaurants and even ran to a smart dance-restaurant and a casino on top of the hill. Some Swedish visitors came aboard for drinks and we had a jolly evening. Although it was a Sunday and the shops were shut, our friends managed to call up a bookseller who obligingly opened his shop to sell me some Norwegian charts for the next day's leg.

We had expected a visit from the Swedish Customs at Stroemstad, but none came and no one seemed any the worse for it. It was blowing a little from the WSW. that morning, but we felt that a passage of the more sheltered leads northwards would not bring us to any harm. And so we left Swedish waters and for the first time in my boat's life we ran up the Norwegian flag. There was some talk of putting into Fredrikstad, which the guide-book seemed to recommend, but we decided in the end to push on to Hankoe. One always feels one must have been once to all these famous yachting places, so as to be able to hold one's own at the dinner-table later. Hankoe was, in fact, a very beautiful anchorage. We were, with one exception, the only yacht in commission there and we spent a beautiful care-free night at anchor. But beauty is not all and we could have done with a little more distraction. I was told later that Hankoe in fact only comes to life for one week a year, when the annual regatta is held. We did, however, visit a really first-class—but quite deserted—yacht club ashore, which was the best furnished and equipped I have ever seen.

The Norwegian owner of the other motor yacht at anchor in Hankoe Bay offered to pilot us through a particularly beautiful stretch of leads towards Oslo next morning and I gladly accepted. The scenery, as is so often the case in Norway, was breathtaking. Gone were the smooth grey boulders of the Swedish Skerries. The coastline was redder and the rocks more jagged in these parts and the pine trees came right down to the sea.

I suppose the Oslo Fjord, which one is too inclined to take for granted, offers some of the finest yachting waters in Europe. Certainly the Norwegians know how to make the best use of it. It was crowded with boats of all kinds.

Determined to take what short cuts were possible, I passed through the canal which cuts the little seaport of Moss in two, the bridge obligingly lifting. We soon passed Droebak and its brave forts, 20 miles from Oslo. Just inside, I saw a notice to all shipping entering the Oslo approaches 'This is our bathing-place. Please help to keep it clean', and took a vow not to ditch our gash again until we left. The gentle but virile Norwegians would not appeal in vain.

In Oslo we berthed at the Royal Norwegian Yacht Club at 'Dronningen', where we were made most welcome. The *Norway Pilot*, in its introductory remarks, says 'The Norwegians are essentially a maritime people, and it may be safely said that in no country will British seamen be treated with more kindness, courtesy and honesty than in Norway.'

After our visit to Oslo that summer, I would subscribe wholeheartedly to this opinion. While at 'Dronningen', two great events took place. The King of Norway arrived in his royal yacht *Norge* and my old friend Harry Chisholm-Jack arrived up from England in his *Martinetta* and lay alongside me. On looking through Lloyd's Register together, we agreed that this must be a unique occasion, for both our yachts were registered in Jersey. This seemed a long way away.

All good things—even Norwegian things—have their ending. Life at the

Oslo H.Q. of the Royal Norwegian Yacht Club had been so full of hospitality and pleasure that I found it hard to believe we had been there a week. Johanssen, the club boatman, gave us a magnificent gift of spliced line for the ship's bell and dipped the club's ensign to us as we slid away from the club's 'Dronningen' clubhouse. Anteclimactically, our first stop was only a couple of cables away at a fuelling barge run by 'Esso', where we topped up with duty-free diesel. The barge was anchored conveniently out of the way of commercial shipping in the approaches to Oslo and sold diesel fuel, petrol, lubricants and all the sundries one associates with a first-class fuelling-point, as well as fresh water.

It was a perfect day, flat calm with bright sunshine, and Oslo Fjord presented a remarkable scene as we picked our way down the Hoek Channels through the myriad sailing craft and joined the main leads at Ildjernsflu Light Ship. In Oslo and the other Norwegian ports we visited there were very many sailing boats of most kinds to be seen, but motor yachts were a comparative rarity, even of the smaller kind. We almost never saw one of over 30 ft in length.

The cruise down Oslo Fjord is always delightful, but was never more so than on this summer's day. There was a fair volume of shipping to add to the interest. After passing the Droebak forts, course was altered slightly to starboard to close the western side of the fjord, and at 2015 we entered the little harbour of Aasgaardstrand, a popular summer resort of Oslo people. As, however, the Oslo summer holiday season is usually concentrated on July and the latter part of June, we had the place relatively to ourselves by August 10. This was all the more surprising in that Aasgaardstrand is only a few miles south of the populous Norwegian naval base of Horten, which we had passed close on our starboard hand just previously.

There was an average of about 2 fathoms in the outer part of the harbour and we berthed stern to the quay on the port hand on entering. Aasgaardstrand was well known as the Norwegian version of St Tropez and many people told us of the number of artists that lived and painted there, but I never saw one. The place is famous for the paintings of Edvard Munch, the Norwegian artist who painted a picture called 'Girl on the Bridge', the bridge in question being the inner end of the mole to which we were made fast. This cultural advantage did something to atone for the extreme quiet of the little place.

Next morning we set course 148 for the other side of Oslo Fjord and the Swedish frontier. It was another lovely day. On passage we met up with some fishermen whose acquaintance we made in harbour the previous evening and bought some fish off them. I never care much for cooking fish aboard: it is a messy process involving de-gutting and endless associated smells; but these fish seemed worth it all. Over to starboard we caught sight of the Norwegian whaling fleet at Toensberg, a small town with a vast commercial importance, where the whalers spend their summers, with most of their crews—like the fishermen we had just met—going off inshore fishing on their own account.

There was a bit of sea coming in up the fjord from the southward, but as we got the lee of the numberless frontier islands, this became less noticeable. A boatload of entirely nude people passed us. I remembered with sudden elation that there was a Norwegian nudist colony on one of the islands near Frederikstad and jolly nearly put about. I regret to this day that we missed this chance.

Visibility was excellent coasting southwards, presaging rain. We could clearly see the big lighthouse on Torbjoernskaer islet over to starboard— the normal leading mark for commercial shipping using the Oslo approaches. I thought for a moment of using the inner passage inside the Vaesteron islands, as we had done coming north, but conditions seemed so good that I decided to make the seaward passge. By 1430 we had made Hoernsten Buoy, one of the line of black buoys marking the Swedish-Norwegian frontier and Stroemstad soon lay clearly visible over to port. Scorning a temptation to make this charming little place, I ran up my Swedish courtesy flag in lieu of our old Norwegian friend and put back the ship's clocks one hour, at the same time setting course for the south part of Koster Fjord. Soon the twin pyramids marking the entrance to the narrows of Bissen duly came up and an hour or so later we were passing the picturesque Havstensund. I had half expected at this juncture, where the boat was never more than a few yards from a populated shore, that the Swedish customs would want to know something about us, so we ran up 'Q' just in case. But no one came near us.

On a return passage over much the same waters, it is always nice to visit different ports, so I had decided to make Fjaellbacka that night. The sky was beginning to cloud over and I was glad that we had about enough time to get there before dark. The old familiar seamarks came up. This time Ingrid Bergman was not at home on her island of Dannholm. No flag flew and the windows seemed to be shuttered. The short Swedish summer was ending. We altered to port and entered the lovely fjord leading up to Fjaellbacka. I went stern to the commercial quay and was about to put a gangway when several people came running along to warn us that the mailboat would soon be needing this berth. So we let go and weighed and went over—in a gale of wind with black clouds bearing threateningly down on us—to a small boat harbour, where we made fast alongside in a tropical downpour. This was almost the first serious rain we had met for months and it seemed curiously refreshing.

Fjaellbacka is not a particularly fascinating place, especially in the rain, but the Swedes in it were charming. We made friends with a delightful family, who agreed to join us next day for the trip down the Soten Kanal to Gravarne.

Though the weather was not exactly perfect, it was a joy to be in the pretty canal again. We duly made the signal—two longs and two shorts— asking the one bridge to open for us and it dutifully swung aside. We had intended to visit Smoegen this time—the attractive fishing village on the sound between Kleven and Hasseloen islands, but we did no better here than we had done when northbound. Yachts and fishermen alike make fast alongside, instead of stern to as they should, with the result that there are almost never any berths. The harbour master did his best for us, boarding us to show us first a most exposed berth on the outer mole and secondly a rather depressing basin some way from the town. We thanked him but said 'No' to both these temptations and once again made across the water to Gravarne, where we knew we were assured of a good berth in a protected harbour. No sooner had we settled for the night than we saw our old friend the British motor yacht *Martinetta* approaching from the north channel. We gave them a hand in coming alongside and learned that they had left Oslo very early that morning. I was flattered that her owner had taken my advice and used the leads among the Skerries instead of the open sea passage that he had favoured when northbound. 'What did you think of it?' I asked. He paused for a moment, as all good Scots should before replying to a weighty question. 'I think it was about the most beautiful trip we have ever done.'

Without wanting to look a gift horse in the mouth, I would like to allow myself one criticism of cruising in these waters. It is very difficult, when one goes ashore, to find a rallying-point for one's distractions. There is no 'Bugle Inn', no 'Jolly Sailor', not even a yacht club where one can relax and meet a few friends. The Swedes are friendly and glad of a chance to yarn. They are on the whole gifted with more jollity than the Norwegians, but where can one be jolly? Bars and pubs are non-existent—with the exception of such *mondain* places as Marstrand in summer—and the hotels are usually rather stiff and uninteresting. Democracy has taken this much toll of Swedish life. Some of my Swedish friends told me things were on the mend. I managed at last to clear Customs.

This time there was no trouble at the redoubtable Fisketangen narrows next morning, for we duly did the right thing and left the red buoy to port, which gave 25 ft of water beneath us, instead of practically scraping the bottom as on the way north. There was a little beam sea until we made Lysekil approaches, but thereafter we were in sheltered waters. I had heard a great deal about a little place called Gullholm, about 15 miles south of Lysekil, and we decided to stop here for lunch. It was very well protected and the harbour was fascinating. We climbed the rocks and took one or two photographs. It was not, of course, exactly pulsating with life. I asked what were the local 'sights' and the postmistress's reply was that the cemetery was worth a visit. But the narrow cobbled streets and paths—reminiscent of Lerwick—were a delight.

After lunch the wind died away altogether, so that we were able to take the outer passage down to Marstrand in ideal conditions. When we arrived, however, we were concerned to note a strong current running along the quay to which we were to put our stern. There were quite a few yachts of various nationalities there and I fear I made rather an exhibition of myself in this manoeuvre. The obvious sympathy of the many yachtsmen shouting gratuitous advice from ashore—confirmed later over gin and tonic—did little to help.

Gothenburg-bound next morning, I knew we were in for a bad time of it, for the current was still running strongly and we were wedged in between other yachts and there was a line of buoys to clear without fouling propellers. So I enlisted the help of some of our friends from the previous evening, who took the inshore end of a very long stern line until we had weighed and were able to go ahead and clear the offending buoys. This was the last I saw of Marstrand, a place I shall always recall with pleasure and which I mean to go back to one day.

It was windy coming down to Gothenburg, but there was almost no sea inside the friendly leads and their sheltering islands. We took as many short cuts as possible, arriving in the river $3\frac{1}{2}$ hours after leaving Marstrand. I went at first to the small harbour known as Lilla Bommen on the starboard hand about as far up to the big bridge as possible, but there seemed to be no room. So back we went to Skeppsbroen, where most of the local ferries berth, but the wash of the river craft put up a continuous movement and, dreading an uncomfortable night, I put back to Lilla Bommen, where we finally made fast in the shelter of the stern of the Swedish training ship *Viking*, that was sometimes used at Marstrand as an accommodation ship for the many hundreds of visiting yachtsmen in the regattas.

While at Gothenburg, some journalists came down to see me—I suppose they had heard about our Iron Curtain exploits—and we had what I thought was a rather too hurried interview over drinks. As I feared, my reported remarks next day were almost unrecognizable, but doubtless a good time had been had by all.

At Gothenburg we fuelled, watered, washed decks and had a gas cylinder filled. In Scandinavia, one can get one's gas cylinders—I carry both British and French—filled with great ease. In France it is difficult (unless, of course they are French) and in Italy it is impossible. Evidently, some sort of gas 'Nato' would be a good thing. I have heard of foreign yachts in Italy filling their own cylinders while the Italians ran shrieking from the quay. The gas and the containers are identical, but regulations vary.

In Gothenburg, Customs told us we could get bonded stores at Falkenberg, a day's trip southward, provided we cleared for foreign. I found this news very elating, as our supplies in the world of alcohol were running down dangerously. So we made for Falkenberg with all dispatch. This passage was protected at first by the southern extremities of the West Swedish Skerries, but at Outer Tistlarna, some 15 miles south of Gothenburg, these peter out and the rest is open sea.

An entertaining seamark on passage south was the agglomeration of dangers formed by the small island of Nidingoe and its associated rocks and reefs. These were visible at a great distance, opening up as we approached very close to Lilleland lighthouse and altered course to pass close into Varberg, whence it was an easy run down to the Falkenberg approach buoy. Falkenberg itself is a curious harbour. At the approaches are a series of detached outer moles, with the channel buoys inside them. The inner harbour itself is formed by the dredging of the small river and one lies alongside some rather uninspiring warehouses.

Unlike any other Scandinavian ports we made, the Customs were actually expecting us at Falkenberg and kindly sent down a ship chandler to see to our needs. A tremendous amount of misunderstanding then began. At first all seemed well. There was, it appeared, a bonded store at Halmstad, another port not very far distant, and, if we cared to wait a day or so, stores could be shipped along to us from there. After some thought, we agreed to this plan and filled in a few forms in preparation. Late that evening, however, the ship chandler came back to tell us that it was, after all, impossible for us to be granted bonded stores. There was, he explained, an arrangement between the Scandinavian countries whereby none of them granted bonded facilities to any yacht bound for another Scandinavian harbour. I had already said we were headed for a Danish port. I suppose I could have cheated and said that we were going straight through to Kiel, where the Germans are very reasonable about this sort of thing, but the odds were that we should somehow or other be caught up with, so we accepted our fate with as much good grace as possible. This was not much. The Scandinavian regulations about drink seemed to me quite ridiculous. Why should one be treated differently there from anywhere else? I gathered that, even if we had been the magic figure of 40 tons net or more (a magic 'open Sesame' in England, too) we could not have been sure of getting bonded facilities. Scandinavian yachting friends have explained it to me by saying that (*a*) 'Demon drink' is *persona non grata*, especially in Sweden, where the Socialist Government have great trouble in controlling the manners of their electorate after a couple of drinks, and (*b*) that the Scandinavian Customs have banded together to stop the large amount of cheating that used to go on by self-styled yachts in the smuggling trade. Anyway, it is a great pity, because Scandinavians are the nicest people in the world and ought not to have silly rules to bother them.

There was a beam sea from Falkenberg to the north of Jutland and things were not so comfortable. I meant at first to put into a small but not unknown Danish fishing-port called Gilleleje. We approached it via the Kattegat South lightship and the swept channels indicated on the Danish chart. I really do not know whether one ought still to pay attention to these channels—some 16 years after the last mines could have been laid— but the official advice is 'Do' and mines can be so final.

Gilleleje was packed with fishing-boats and one or two Danish yachts and the harbour master could only offer us an indifferent berth, so we put about and coasted along to Hornbek, another delightful but even smaller harbour. The approach was extremely difficult, especially as work was going on at the harbour mouth, and we as near as not found ourselves aground, but survived, turned on our own axis in the harbour and made fast in the midst of what was, I trust, an admiring crowd.

I flew 'Q' and left it flying for safety, but there did not seem to be any more Customs than there had been in the smaller Swedish ports. Hornbek is cosy and pretty and people are there for one reason only—which is to enjoy themselves. I recommend it. The only snag was that—I suppose due to its miniscule proportions—we were asked to pay Kr. 11 (about 11*s*.) in harbour dues for the one night we were there. This would have been more if, in collusion with the harbour master, we had not cheated about our tonnage. I wish the Danes would not charge so many harbour dues. Otherwise, one can complain of nothing in this remarkable country.

And next day we came home. That is, to our Danish home port of Skovshoved. To our favourite berth, with the fresh water alongside, and the harbour master who was also the Customs man and who made every- thing easy for us. And to a fuel pump all ready to serve and to our friends at the Royal Danish Yacht Club and to a happy ending to a cruise up the Skerries and back that I shall never forget.

Somehow, that September, I must get home to Jersey from Copenhagen. Many of my Danish friends, including that veteran Freddie Wessel, who was also lying at Skovshoved in his *Dania II*, did their best to persuade me to winter in Denmark. Viggo Jarl, another great Danish yachtsman, had his *Atlantide* lying at Humlebaek up the Sound and kindly introduced me to the local yard. Freddie was all for wintering in Svendborg, a port where I had made my first Danish landfall many years ago. Their counsels nearly prevailed. But a sense of continuing adventure, together with the fact that I like to have my boat at home in Jersey with me for the winter when I can, finally persuaded me to sail while the sun still shone. Which way was one to go home?

17. Copenhagen to Hamburg via the Elbe-Lübeck Canal

I was really tired of the Kiel Canal. Things that are the most convenient (as, indeed, the Kiel Canal must be admitted to be) are not always the greatest fun for a yacht. And so it was that I decided there and then to take the canal across north-west Germany that leads you from Lübeck to the River Elbe.

One can hardly call this a short cut. It is about three times as long as taking the Kiel Canal itself, but it has the merit of novelty and takes you for some miles alongside the zonal frontier between West and East Germany, always a curious and tantalizing experience.

Saying farewell to the hospitable yacht basin at Skovshoved, just north of Copenhagen, we set course for the little old Dutch-built harbour of Dragör, just south of the capital, where we spent a crowded but quiet night. The 75-mile run next day through the Boegestroem via Kallehave, under the great Storstroem Bridge (Europe's longest), and thence into the Guldborgsund for a night in Guldborg itself, was accomplished in radiant sunshine. So hot was it that we could not resist the temptation to anchor for a swim near Kallehave, thus arriving too late in the Guldborgsund to proceed on up to Nyköbing F. And so, sounding a long and a short and flying flag N to make the bridge open, we made fast for a night's rest.

The channel in the South Guldborg Sound has to be taken very slowly even in a vessel like mine drawing not more than 5 ft of water. You must have the Danish chart aboard and follow the broomstick-marked fairway religiously. The bottom is partly rock. Off Gedser, however, your troubles end and, making the southern approach buoy, we were able to set course via the indicated swept channels for Lübeck Bay. A night at Neustadt, thence to Travemünde.

We finally sailed inland from Travemünde late one September afternoon, having cautiously lowered our masts beforehand. It was a curious sensation. To starboard all ashore was normal. Trains puffed along, people swam and fished, lights shone. To port, soon after sailing, all was dead. Grim notices on dolphins marking the river channel warned us that over there was the Soviet Zone and that this was the frontier. Over on the Communist side was no sign of life.

The yacht ploughed her way silently upriver. On the Soviet side of the estuary could now be made out the terrifying watch-towers overshadowing the strip of river on our port hand. In the gathering dusk we could not quite make out whether these were manned or not, but we could clearly see the strip of carefully-raked earth in the ploughed-up belt of land all along inside the frontier.

We made Lübeck soon after last light. I was glad we had lowered our masts, as we were thus able to pass under the only river bridge without delay. The Lübeck Hochbruecke raised itself when I shone my searchlight on it and we passed beneath to our berth in the Klughafen for the night. Lübeck is a charming old Hanseatic city, full of priceless monuments, and it was not difficult to fill the evening.

Thick fog delayed our departure next morning from Lübeck and, even after sailing an hour later than I had intended, we had to make fast for another hour on the outskirts of the city to wait for it to lift. At the first lock there was a considerable delay, which we learned later was due to insufficient water in the canal. This caused the locks to be opened only when a commercial vessel presented herself. Otherwise, the keepers had instructions to open only at intervals of one hour.

I was therefore rather surprised when I was told that, by paying an extra DM. 1.50 per lock (we had already paid a passage fee of DM. 7—for the seven-lock passage), we could secure a special opening. Fortunately, we with our draught of 1.50 m. just fitted into the permitted maximum draught that day of 1.70 m. Normally, the permitted maximum draught was 2.50 m. We observed that the regulations on this German canal were very much more closely observed than on the French.

For instance, a slight argument with a somewhat surly lock-keeper at one of the locks had an unexpected result. We had, I admit, been going a trifle faster than the permitted 6 km. an hour. At the next lock a policeman boarded us and told me that he had timed our speed from lock to lock, which he made out as 10.8 km. per hour. I was a bit shaken to hear this and wondered how he could possibly have taken such trouble as to find out. Over a drink, however, he confided in me that it was our friend the sour-tempered lock-keeper who had 'complained'. I suppose it was his idea of getting even with us.

Despite these alarms, however, we were able to put the 44 miles from Lübeck to Lauenburg, at the entrance to the River Elbe, astern of us that day, a matter of some 9 hours of navigation. There were only seven locks, but it took some time to negotiate each of them. At the last lock, that at Lauenburg itself, we had been told that it only opened every 3 hours, so we were greatly relieved when we sailed straight into it. There was a considerable volume of traffic on the canal, much more than when I last used it some five years ago, but, as usual on European waterways, everyone was most helpful.

At Lauenburg we were again very close to the zonal frontier. There was here not only a road and rail frontier post, but also a river frontier control post just a short way up the River Elbe from the point where we berthed for the night at the junction of river and canal. Lauenburg itself was a picturesque little town and the walk alongside the Elbe by moonlight was enchanting.

It was annoying to be woken next morning soon after six o'clock by a sand-hopper wanting our berth for construction work. Rather than shift, I decided to sail downriver at once. Passage at first was easy. There seemed to be plenty of water in the river despite the season and the middle channel was easily distinguishable by the groins which ran towards it from either bank. Last time I had come down the Elbe the river had been in flood and it was far from easy to see the way.

The Elbe in these upper reaches is not easy to navigate. There is little to mark the channels and several times we found ourselves hard and fast aground; fortunately the bottom everywhere was sand. This was probably due at least in part to its being low water at Hamburg. After twice going aground in this rather humiliating way, I decided to eat humble pie and we followed in the wake of a slow-moving barge. From the many twists and turns he made, without any apparent rhyme or reason, it became clear to us just how tortuous the river channel was. At midday we passed beneath the great Hohenzollern Bridge at Hamburg and by lunch-time, having cleared the Free Port Customs, we were fast at the Uebersee Bridge and raised our masts again.

I can recommend the Lübeck-Elbe Canal route to other yachtsmen wishing to make a more interesting passage across north-western Germany than via the standard Kiel Canal route. From Travemünde to Hamburg is approximately two days of normal navigation, which is about the same as—or even slightly less than—if you were to take the Kiel route to Hamburg. For here you would have to reckon on the tides which sweep up and down the Elbe. Even if there is no intention of making Hamburg and all that is required is a passage across Germany to make the North Sea homewards, the Lübeck–Elbe route is worth considering if your dimensions permit. At a guess, and with normal water conditions, I would say that these were about: Length, 150 ft; draught, 9 ft; freeboard, 15 ft; beam, 30 ft.

On Going Foreign

*Do's and Don't's for the Seaborne Tyro
with a list of places where to buy foreign charts*

A yachtsman has not lived up to his title until he has 'been foreign'. Unfortunately, many people think that to take a yacht abroad is a major difficulty. They imagine fierce Customs men 'rummaging' their way from stem to stern, the crew meanwhile held prisoner in the forecastle, or preparing lists of misdemeanours carrying giant fines. Bellicose policemen lurk behind every bollard. Cohorts of petty officials, armed with sheaves of unintelligible forms, perch like vultures on the pierheads, ready to attack the innocent mariner and tear him to shreds.

It is not at all like that. Of course, things are strange, but isn't that part of the fun? Generally speaking, a British yachtsman going foreign has fewer horrors to face than a foreign yachtsman visiting our shores. The Continentals exercise their control in a more leisurely, less apparent way than we do. But they know what goes on, just the same.

The journey, naturally, requires preparation. Obviously passports are needed, though in none of the countries close to these islands are visas necessary. In larger yachts, which are sometimes apt to be treated like merchantmen, it is not strictly necessary for all the crew to have passports; a list of the crew who have 'signed on' for the voyage can be made out on a special form issued by the Ministry of Transport and known as an A.3 Form. When this is shown to the foreign authorities they simply give each man named on it a permit to go ashore in the precincts of the port and do not bother about passports. These forms can be obtained from the shipping offices in all major British ports and from our consular representatives abroad. It is certainly not worth while for a small yacht to bother about this 'signing on' except when she proposes visiting rather unusual places. For instance, when I cruised to East Germany and Poland in 1959, I made sure, when I got to Hamburg, that we were all 'signed on' on an A.3, so that were we to disappear completely to the salt-mines there would at least be some official record of our having done so! When I visit the Black Sea, I shall take care to do the same thing.

The ship herself needs identification. If she possesses a Certificate of British Registry, and it is strongly recommended that she should, this will be ample evidence and is universally accepted. Countries which issue temporary documents to enable the yacht to minimize formalities while coasting in their waters (such as Greece, Italy and Yugoslavia) will accept this as a basic document. There have been instances of yachts being stolen or having writs attached to them. To carry your certificate of registry will show that yours is not one of them. I remember arriving at Paimpol, in Brittany, some seasons ago while there was a hue and cry on for a motor yacht like mine that had disappeared from the Channel Islands while under writ. It was not until our certificate of registry had been duly vetted that the French Customs became their normal pleasant selves.

If she has no certificate of registry, she may be tempted to sail from her U.K. base on the strength of possessing the Revenue Form 29(Sale) and 30(Sale), both of which ensure that she is immune from any British import duties on return. But the purpose of this document is not to act as a yacht's 'passport' and it is questionable whether it will always, or, indeed, ever, be acceptable for foreign authorities. I strongly recommend every yachtsman to secure a Certificate of British Registration and never to rely on any other papers. By law, in fact, every vessel of over 15 tons net should be registered if going foreign, a fact which is sometimes forgotten. An unregistered vessel abroad is, moreover, not entitled to the protection of her flag.

So the passports and the Certificates of British Registry are all a yacht requires in the way of papers when going foreign in western Europe. In France, on arrival at the first port, the 'green book' (passport for the yacht) must be obtained from the Customs. If she means to navigate inland waterways in France, Belgium, Germany or the Netherlands, she may be asked to go through the same drill as a car used to undergo. That is, she may be asked to deposit a bond at the port of entry, equivalent to her value. This can usually be arranged through a local bank, which will get into touch with the owner's bank at home and so produce the required guarantee. But a simpler way around all this is merely to get an international '*Carnet de Passages en Douane*' from the A.A. or R.A.C. before starting, just the same as with a car.

It is never certain that these papers will be needed, but they sometimes are. Questions of this kind only arise if the yacht actually enters the country concerned; she can, for instance, go as far as Rouen up the Seine, or well into Belgium, Holland and through the Kiel Canal without technically 'entering' the countries concerned at all. In point of fact, the French never ask for a deposit for yachts going up to Paris and down again, and on two occasions I have even crossed the whole of France by canal without this question being raised. But on other occasions I have had to produce my papers, so it is as well to be prepared.

Money matters are much less of a problem than they used to be.

It sometimes happens that repairs are needed while abroad. Have no fear. Shipyards abound and the Continental mechanic usually does a first-class job and is often far more '*débrouillard*' than his British counterpart; which means that he can make bricks with very little straw. Be sure, however, to agree on the charges first, as far as possible.

Charts are important. The Admiralty charts, which are available in almost every major port, are, in my opinion, far better than the various 'yachting charts' now being produced. But neither the Admiralty charts nor those privately produced will show the necessary detail of all the complicated inshore passages in foreign countries. I found it quite impossible, for instance, to navigate in the 'Riddle of the Sands' areas inside the Friesians on Admiralty charts. The Dutch and German charts, which can be bought in almost every port along that coast, are an absolute *sine qua non*. The same applied when I navigated the west coast of Sweden. Only the local Swedish charts are really complete. In Danish waters it is a moot point whether our own Admiralty charts are sufficient: personally, I think they are. In Norway, however, I would not care to navigate the inner leads unless I had the Norwegian local charts.

The chance of running on a wartime mine is now remote for a yacht. The cautious will nevertheless like to arm themselves with the Admiralty's

routeing instructions to merchant ships (short title: NEMEDRI) which
can be obtained from most shipping offices. They show the swept channels
clearly, especially for the Friesian and Danish waters. The NEMEDRI
chartlets and instructions can be of considerable value in that they often
indicate sea-marks not shown on the normal charts.

In addition to charts of the seaways, there are excellent maps produced
(mostly in Paris) which show the course of the principal French rivers. I
have used these for the Seine, the Marne, the Yonne and the Saône. For
the Rhône, a pilot is essential and a map, except for one's own interest, is
not needed. Some of the Belgian rivers have been treated in this way and
I can recommend the maps, too. For the Rhine, the best publication is
Swiss, though rather difficult to get hold of. There are various maps of the
Dutch waterways, none of them quite satisfactory: use Admiralty charts
where possible.

When navigating the French inland waterways, especially the great
canal network, the only reliable publications are those officially compiled
by the French Government. These consist of detailed maps and accompanying guide-books.

Duty-free stores are more readily available 'foreign' than in Britain to a
small yacht. There is none of the irritating application of the 'Over
40 tons' rule; size of the vessel plays no part. Duty-free stores are available
to a visitor at almost every major French port, and there is no attempt to
prohibit their consumption in harbour (except possibly on the Riviera,
where there has been a certain amount of cheating). In Belgian ports, one
is almost forced to buy something! The Dutch tend to approximate their
British colleagues and are more severe in their application of the rules,
while the Germans are very easy-going. The Scandinavians have had a lot
of trouble with smugglers and do not issue duty-free stores to yachts below
40 tons net, as in Britain. Scandinavian yachts thus make frequent visits to
Kiel for stocking up and the Danish and Swedish Customs are unfortunately thus kept rather too much on the *qui vive*. The result is that they
like to know just how much a foreigner is carrying, although, even after
sealing, they are very reasonable about issuing it whenever called upon. In
the Mediterranean, conditions are very lax. But do not be misled into
thinking the local people don't know what is going on.

Do not forget the courtesy flags of the countries the yacht is going to visit.

Where a burgee is worn at the masthead, it is correct to wear the courtesy flag at the starboard yard. A hoist of the yacht's distinguishing letters looks nice on entering harbour, but is by no means essential. Pay great attention to flags and see that 'colours' and 'sunset' are done at the right time. The yacht is an ambassador. And don't forget to take a 'Q' flag and fly it until the yacht has been given 'pratique'; in some French ports they ask for it to be hauled down as soon as they come aboard, generally because they are too lazy to give proper clearance. But it is in every yachtsman's interest to fly it until after the formalities are over. A drink and a cigarette in the saloon are, by the way, much appreciated by the foreign officials, many of whom lead dreary lives. One can do much good this way.

I had almost forgotten the Admiralty Pilot Books, obtainable from all nautical bookstores. Though written for larger ships, much of the information they contain applies equally to yachts and none should venture far without them. One more point; if a visit is made to a foreign yacht club—especially the more distant ones—there is nothing they like more than to receive a burgee of the visiting yacht's club. Maybe they will give one of theirs in return. So take a few burgees—if they are a wee bit tattered, so much the better. *'Bon Voyage!'*

FOREIGN CHARTS AND PLANS

France

Charts: For the more obscure areas such as the River Rance and the Chausey Islands, French charts are essential, but generally speaking our own Admiralty charts are the most reliable and are more easily read. French yachtsmen, indeed, often prefer British charts. French charts are obtainable at better-class *librairies* at major French ports: if they are needed before leaving U.K., it is suggested that they be ordered from:

Société d'Editions Geographiques Maritimes et d'Outremer, S.A., 17 Rue Jacob, Paris, 6.

Plans: The most reliable are the official plans and guides, published on behalf of the French Government in two volumes and entitled *Guide Officiel de la Navigation Interieure*. These show the plans of all the principal French inland waterways in great detail and can be obtained by writing to either of the following:

Editions Berger-Levrault, 5 Rue August-Comte, Paris, 6.

Girard et Barrère, 17 Rue de Buci, Paris, 6.

The latter supply an excellent detailed map (in four coloured sections forming one sheet) of the French waterways—and some Belgian—entitled *Carte des Canaux de la France et de la Belgique*.

In addition, there are a number of very practical, though sometimes rather inaccurate, folding plans of the main French rivers which can be bought from any of the above, but can also often be bought at

Captain O. M. Watts Ltd,
49 Albemarle Street, London, W.1.

Some excellent guides to the smaller French ports and anchorages, often just those that a yacht requires, published under the title of *Guides de Petite Croisière*, by Editions 'Eole', 25 Rue de Valois, Paris. More detailed pilotage books, containing charts based on the official British or French charts with soundings and leading marks are Adlard Coles's *Channel Harbours* (Barfleur to St Malo), *North Brittany Harbours and Anchorages* and *Biscay Harbours and Anchorages*, Parts I and II, obtainable from Captain O. M. Watts and booksellers.

Belgium
Belgian charts may be bought in Ostende at the quayside *librairie*, but, in my view, British charts are more than adequate.

For plans of the Belgian waterways, apply to:
Messrs W. Seghers,
Franklin Rooseveltplaats, 9, Antwerp.

Netherlands
Dutch charts are seldom better for Dutch waters than their British counterpart, except for the navigation in the Friesian shoal waters, where they are a necessity. They are also desirable for the Ijsselmeer (Zuider Zee). On arrival in the country, they are easily bought at almost any specialist bookshop. If desired in advance

of arrival, it is suggested that inquiries be made of:

Bureau voor Watertoerisme,
Keizersgracht, 590, Amsterdam, C.

This bureau can help with both charts and plans of the very complicated system of the Netherlands inland waterways. This applies also to the Rhine.

Denmark
Danish chart agents, in common with most of their colleagues in the other Scandinavian countries, will supply not only Danish charts but also Swedish and Norwegian. It is suggested that application be made to:

L. Nilsson, Shipchandler,
Nyhavn, 31(h), Copenhagen.

Germany
German charts are essential for the shoal waters of the Friesians, but all other German North Sea waters are adequately covered by our own Admiralty charts. For the inshore German waters of the Baltic, however, German charts are also very desirable. East Germany publishes its own charts of East German waters.

For charts apply to:

United Baltic Corporation G.m.b.H.,
Kiel-Holtenau.

For plans of Inland Waterways, apply to:

'Rhein' Verlagsgesellschaft m.b.H.,
Postfach 142, Duisburg.

Sweden
If arriving direct from the U.K., the best plan is probably to ask the local yacht club, though it may be assumed that most

good booksellers also stock them. If required before sailing, application for information can be made to:

The Secretary, Kungl. Svenska Segel
   Sällskapet,

Birger Jarlsgatan, 4, Stockholm.

Norway

Good booksellers stock local charts. If
required in advance of arrival, application can be made to:

The Secretary, Kongelig Norsk
   Seilforening,

Fridtjof Nansen's Plass, 9(iii), Oslo.

From a Traveller's Scrapbook

In case it may be of practical help, I have made this list of people and things in places I have visited. It is possible that a small percentage (though not much) may have been overtaken by the march of time, in which case I crave forgiveness. All wakes fade, even that of Odysseus.

France
The principal water routes across France are:
1. Le Havre to Marseille via the Bourbonnais Route (Canal du Centre, etc.): 179 locks and 550 sea-miles.
2. Le Havre to Marseille via River Marne Route: 162 locks and 570 sea-miles.
3. Le Havre to Marseille via Burgundy Route: 255 locks and 505 sea-miles.
4. The Midi Route (Sète to Bordeaux via Toulouse): 118 locks and 232 sea-miles. The Canal de Jonction—between La Nouvelle and a point on the Midi Canal west of Béziers, is 7 km. long and has six locks.

The average fast passages (working most days from 0630 to 1900 and not stopping for meals) are:
1. Bourbonnais Route: 16 days.
2. Marne Route: 15 days.
3. Burgundy Route: 14 days.
4. Midi Route: 7 to 8 days (Sète to Bordeaux).

Chômages (Period during which some of the pounds are closed for cleaning the canals):
1. Midi Route: Few days in April and few days in June.
2. Other canal routes: Usually in July and/or August. It is wise to make inquiries in advance.

Diesel fuel resembling normal marine diesel may usually be bought inside France at about 2s. 0d. per gallon.

French River Pilotage:
1. THE RHÔNE
M. Joseph Pariset,
17 Place Paul Nas,
La Mulatière, Lyon.
Tel.: 512983 or 512579.
M. Henri Morvent,
59 Rue du Fort St Irenée, Lyon, 5.
Tel.: 276348.
M. Ferdinand Marel,
50 Chemin de la Synagogue, Avignon.
Tel.: 810023.

M. Albin Gelgenbacher,
10 Quai Rimbaud, Lyon.
M. Kléber Lorio,
20 Rue Stephane Deschant,
La Mulatière, Lyon.

2. THE SAÔNE

M. Pierre Thurillet,
6 Quai St Cosme,
Chalon-sur-Saône.
Tel.: 673.
M. Georges Pennequin,
26 Quai St Cosme,
Chalon-sur-Saône.
Tel.: 1247.
M. Coulon.
Tel.: Tournus 257.

3. THE DOUBS

M. Jean Seger,
Ile-sur-le-Doubs, Doubs.
Tel.: Ile-sur-le-Doubs 84.

River Pilotage Fees: These tend to rise continuously and are, in any case, often subject to modification by argument. The following rates give a rough idea:

I. THE RHÔNE

Lyon to Arles: About NF. 150.
Lyon to Avignon: About NF. 120.
Avignon to Arles: About NF. 50.
Arles to Lyon (upstream): About NF. 400, plus keep on passage.

2. THE SAÔNE

Chalon-sur-Saône to Lyon: NF. 100, with an extra payment of about NF. 20 if piloted through the city of Lyon.

3. THE DOUBS

Dôle to Ile-sur-le-Doubs: About NF. 300, subject to time and distance.

French Inland Waterways Publications:
1. The official waterway guide entitled *Guide Officiel de la Navigation Intérieure* gives all the information required, including maps. It is in two volumes and may be had from:
Editions Berger-Levrault,
5 Rue August-Comte, Paris, 6.

2. Another official publication entitled *Carte des Canaux de la France et de la Belgique*—in four coloured sections forming one sheet—is an excellent detailed waterways map, obtainable from:
Messrs Girard et Barrère,
17 Rue de Buci, Paris, 6.

3. Folding plans of the *Rivers, Seine, Marne, Yonne, Saône and Rhône* are published by:
Messrs Société d'Editions Géographiques, Maritimes et d'Outremer,
17 Rue Jacob, Paris, 6,
who also sell an excellent one-sheet plan of all the main French waterways, which may sometimes be used instead of (2) above.

Driving Licence (or *Certificat de Capacité*). This is seldom required, but if playing for safety, one may be had from:
Secretary, Yacht and Motor Boat Association,
90 Bedford Court Mansions, London, W.C.1.

Minimum Lock Dimensions (with freeboard beneath bridges):
1. *Paris to Lyon via Bourbonnais Route:*
   Length   39 metres.
   Beam   5.12 metres.
   Draught   2 metres.
   Freeboard 3.5 metres.
2. *Paris to Lyon via River Marne Route:*
   Length   38.3 metres.

Beam   5.1 metres.
Draught   2 metres.
Freeboard   3.5 metres.
3. *Paris to Lyon via Burgundy Route:*
Length   39 metres.
Beam   5.2 metres.
Draught   2 metres.
Freeboard   3.4 metres.
4. *Bordeaux to Sète via Midi Route:*
Length   30 metres.
Beam   5.5 metres.
Draught   1.8 metres.
Freeboard   3.5 metres.
5. *Lyon to Strasbourg or Basle:*
Length   38.70 metres.
Beam   5.08 metres.
Draught   2 metres.
Freeboard   3.48 metres.

As the above are the minimum measurements of the *lock* (and headroom beneath bridges), it is wise to leave a bit to spare when calculating possibilities of passage.

Some Useful Addresses:

France
LE HAVRE
Ship Chandler:
Messrs General Stores,
Place Saint-Vincent-de-Paul.
Tel.: 23552.

PARIS
Touring Club de France,
Port de Plaisance de Paris,
Quai de la Conférence, Paris, 8.
Tel.: Anjou 2880.

LYON
Rhône River Authority,
Bureau de l'Ingénieur en Chef,
9 Rue Grolée, Lyon.
Tel.: Franklin 0928.
Ponts et Chaussées,

Service de Navigation Rhône-Saône et
    Canal du Rhône au Rhin,
12 Rue Port-du-Temple, Lyon, 2.
Tel.: Gailleton 5583.

ARLES
Office National de la Navigation,
Quai de Trinquetaille, Arles.
Tel.: 085.
Director: M. J. Dayre.
Boatyards:
Chantiers Barriol. Tel. 697.
M. Jacques Bourdignon. Tel. 322.

ROUEN
Shipping and Transit Agent:
Agence Maritime Herpin et Cie.,
22 Rue Georges d'Amboise, Rouen.
Tel.: 714346.

MARSEILLE
Yacht Chandler:
Captain George Jochumsen,
74 Quai du Port.
Tel.: 204080.

Transit Agency:
Transports P. Sapte et Cie.,
28 Rue de la République.
Tel.: 209444.

Yacht Brokers:
Yacht Mediterranée,
96 Quai du Port.
Tel.: 207393.

Tows on the Rhône:
Compagnie Générale de Navigation,
Havre, Paris, Lyon, Marseille (known as H.P.L.M.),
5 Quai de la Joliette.
Tel.: Colbert 0409.
Directeur: M. Tardieu.
(Lyon Office Telephone Franklin 5515.)
Towage Fees from NF. 700.
Citerna.

Marseille telephone number Colbert
8963.
Directeur: M. Corbin.
Lyon telephone number Parmentier 6534.
Directeur: M. Hermet.
Towage fees from NF. 800.
Monsieur Réné Olivier, an independent
barge-owner, of 23 Quai J. B. Simon,
Fontaines-sur-Saône, Rhône, also under-
takes towage at approximately the same
fees as the above.

CANNES

The principal yacht agencies on the Côte
d'Azur are located here and are:
Agence Camper and Nicholsons Ltd,
30–31 La Croisette.
Tel.: 393928.
Agence A. Glémot et Cie.,
18 Quai St Pierre.
Tel.: 390472.
Agence Maritime Internationale,
12 Quai St Pierre.
Tel.: 394044.
M. Gérard Yven,
21 Quai St Pierre.
Tel.: 391974.

ANTIBES
Agency:
Agence du Port,
30 Rue Aubernon.
Tel.: 342710.

TOULOUSE
Canal Navigation Permits and information obtainable from:
Monsieur l'Ingenieur en Chef des Ponts
et Chaussées,
Service des Canaux du Midi et Latéral à
la Garonne,
Ponts et Chaussées,
2 Port St Etienne, Toulouse.

BORDEAUX
Shipwrights and Mechanics:
Messrs G. Mounerat et F. Gaussens,
99 Rue Bourbon (at Bacalan Basin).
Tel.: 443982.
Constructions Navales A. Bugaret,
Quai de Queyrie,
Bordeaux-Bastide (across river from
town).
Tel.: 922790.
Ship Chandler:
Fin Arnesen and Son Ltd,
4 Rue Lafayette.
Tel.: 480177.
Laundry:
Blanchisserie du Port,
33 Quai des Chartrons.
Tel.: 484196.
Bordeaux Yacht Club is situated downstream
from the city on the left bank at a place
named Point du Jour. It can accom-
modate vessels of up to 50 ft in length at
pontoons and the staff is informative and
obliging.

ROYAN
A yacht basin was in construction in 1965.

LA ROCHELLE
Shipwrights and Mechanics:
Paboul Frères,
Rue des Chantiers de Construction.
Tel.: 3199.
Radiomechanics and Electricians:
Téchnique et Radio,
3, bis, Avenue de Strasbourg.
Tel.: 3368.
Fuel:
Société Française des Pétroles B.P.
Tel.: 2552.
Slipping Careening, etc.:
Messrs Bolcioni et Cie.

Yacht Club:
Société des Régates de la Rochelle.
Tel.: 4447 or 4782.

LES SABLES D'OLONNE

The representation at the Touring Club de France, 13 Rue E. Delvaut, is excellent.

LORIENT

The ship chandler, M. Pierre Sicaud, 10 Rue de Carnel (Tel.: 643088), will arrange for fuel to be supplied.

DOUARNENEZ

Mechanics:
Messrs A. Vigouroux,
Rue du Mole.
Tel.: 408.

BREST

Ship Chandler:
M. Jean Fournier,
32 Quai de la Douane.
Tel.: 443647.

MORLAIX

Yacht Club de Morlaix. The commodore, Dr Jean Pillet, is available at 20 Quai de Tréguier (Tel.: 659). Fresh water is available at the lock, which opens 2 hours before H.W. and closes 1 hour after H.W.

Germany and the Rhine

A. THE RHINE

Basle to Rotterdam via the Oude Maas 880 km. (about 470 sea-miles).

Time under way 52 hours (very much more, of course, if going upstream).

Prices of diesel fuel (all duty-free) (as at end 1957)
In France   NF. 0.19 per litre
In Germany DM. 0.16½ per litre

Pilotage Fees:
Fessenheim to Strasbourg: S.Frs 35 plus S.Frs 2 per hour's waiting.
Strasbourg to Mannheim: DM. 42.50, no journey money, and DM. 2 per hour waiting.
Mannheim to Mainz: DM. 35 and DM. 2 per hour waiting, and no journey money.
Bingen to St Goar: DM. 20 and no journey money.

Minimum Depth of River in normal year:
Duisburg-Ruhrort to the sea   7 ft 3 in.
Cologne to Duisburg-Ruhrort   6 ft.
St Goar to Cologne   7 ft.
Karlsruhe to St Goar   5 ft 6 in.
Strasbourg to Karlsruhe   5 ft.
Basle to Strasbourg
(non-canalized section)   4 ft.

(*Note.*—By 1967, it is expected that the entire section from Basle to Strasbourg will have been canalized, thus greatly increasing this depth.)

Least Clearance of Bridges:
Rotterdam to Mannheim
   8.96 metres (or 29 ft 3 in.).
Mannheim to Strasbourg
   5.75 metres (or 18 ft 9 in.).
Strasbourg to Basle
   3.38 metres (or 11 ft 2 in.).

Recommended Contacts on Passage:
Rotterdam: Alex. Paton's Shipstores, Veerhaven 12. Tel.: 20036. (For stores, repairs and advice.)
Cologne: Herr Theodor Weber, Messrs Weber-Schiff, Leystapel, 39. Tel.: 211728. (For advice and repairs, etc.)

Also the various offices of the Schweizerische Reederei A.G. *en route*: these are listed in the text of Chapter 1.

B. THE KIEL CANAL AND BALTIC

Agency for Passage of Kiel Canal:
United Baltic Corporation, G.m.b.H.,
Brunsbuettelkoog (Tel.: 512).
Kiel-Holtenau (Tel.: Kiel 31302).

Ship Chandlers for Kiel Canal:
Messrs Christensen and Samsoe.
Kiel (Tel.: 36698).
Brunsbuettelkoog (Tel.: 464).

Canal Dues:
These are minimal: I paid DM. 22 for a
single passage for my 32 gross ton yacht.
There was a handling charge of DM. 0.5
and no pilot was required.

TRAVEMUENDE
Ship Chandler:
Carl Bartelsen, Vorderreihe, 8.
Tel.: 2151.

Shipyard:
Alfred Hagelstein.
Tel.: 2171.

LUEBECK
Ship Chandler:
Armin von Hoerschelmann.
Tel.: 26106.

Index